On Your Mark,

Get Set,

Go-Live!

The SMART Approach to
Implementing SAP®

Dan Raven

DEDICATION

I would like to dedicate this book to my loving wife, Karen, and my three daughters, Sarah, Michelle, and Amanda who have supported my work life and have been the reason for me to balance it with a fantastic home life.
I love you all very much.

I would also like to dedicate this book to my parents who have been very encouraging my whole life and who urged me to write this book.

This book was written in memory of Mindie Prom (Thida Ea), who was a great friend and the best data migration expert I ever knew. She was an amazing analyst. She was beyond dedicated and gave her all to everything she undertook. She was brilliant. She was inspirational. She will never be forgotten by anyone lucky enough to have known her.

Preface

"A mediocre idea that generates enthusiasm will go further than a great idea that inspires no one."

– Mary Kay Ash

People act in disbelief when I tell them that we roll out SAP® in only 2 months to newly acquired manufacturing plants.

This book will make you a believer because, not only will I discuss in detail the many manufacturing plants that have been brought up on SAP using this method, but I will share the detailed project plan and cut-over plan. I will share examples of those and other documents including presentations and issue logs. This book is filled with tips & tricks used along the way. This book is not only meant to be a step-by-step handbook to a speedy ERP implementation, but it is also designed to be a reference guide. One can easily refer to sections that apply to a particular stage of a project.

I will also explain what is required to create an environment for a successful implementation. From company politics to the set up of the war room, this book will show you how to create an environment for a successful implementation.

I have heard many skeptics who say things like, "It may work for a small company, but not for one as large as ours", or "This kind of implementation would not work at a company like ours" or "Our business is too complex for a fast implementation". The fact is this method has been used during more than 10 successful SAP implementations with companies of various sizes and complexities. One of the most important ingredients is a positive attitude. Please keep an open mind while consuming the contents of this book. This approach has been proven to be successful many times with varying SAP teams. It is repeatable. This book provides the tools you need to make it happen for your company as well.

People who should read this book:

People who are involved at any capacity in an ERP implementation (project managers, project team members, business champions / key users) as well as managers who are running a company that plans to implement an ERP application. Presidents, CEOs, CIOs, CTOs, CFOs, and COOs who want to implement an ERP application for their companies in the most cost effective way, which happens to be the most efficient way to standardize business processes such as order-to-cash and procure-to-pay throughout your company. IT Managers and Project Managers who want to learn a step-by-step approach to ensure a successful ERP implementation while creating an environment to sustain and support an application that will be undergoing constant improvements.

Table of Contents

Chapter 1
The Starting Line

"Whatever you can do, or dream you can, Begin it. Boldness has genius, power and magic, Begin it now."
                                                           – Johnann Wolfgang von Goethe

Even in a race against time, there has to be a starting line. If the starting point is not defined then one will never know if they beat the record. In a project, the starting point has to be well defined also. But I will cover the starting point of the project in Chapter 3 "The Project Preparation".

I would like to begin this book by enlightening you with some background which will provide a context for realizing this method of ERP (Enterprise Resource Planning) system implementations. First, my experience in ERP implementations is with SAP. I have over 15 years of experience implementing SAP. While working for SMART Modular Technologies, Inc., a high-tech manufacturer in Silicon Valley, I implemented SAP in 15 design, manufacturing and distribution centers around the world.

In the beginning we had four manufacturing plants (located in California, Puerto Rico, Scotland, and Malaysia) each running on a different instance of FourthShift® accounting software. We configured SAP 3.1h for these plants in a project that lasted 8 months. We went live in our California facility on February 4, 1999 at 2:30AM. Then we brought up our plants in Scotland, Puerto Rico, and Malaysia in intervals of 3 months. As a team we supported each site in a post-go-live support mode for one month before starting the next implementation.

Now, you could say, "Wait a minute. That's cheating. You had already configured the system for all four of your factories during the 8 month project." And you would be correct – for the most part. Actually, we had a problem with our facility in Penang, Malaysia where we had configured the company in MYR (Malaysian Ringgits) but before go-live, it was decided it should have been configured in USD. (Now we have a way of determining the proper currency to use early in the process, which I will share in Chapter 2 "The SMART Approach".) But for now it is only important to know that this caused issues in the SAP configuration that could not be resolved. We had to abandon the company code and start over again configuring the Penang plant with a new company code, plant, and sales organization.

We had only 2 months to re-create Penang in our system, load the data, test the system, train the users and go-live. Therefore, Penang was our first true 2 month SAP implementation.

Let's take a step back. In 1998 & 1999, we were a young fresh team. We did not know SAP very well and relied heavily on our consultants. SAP had already developed the ASAP methodology, but had not developed the High Tech solution nor the out-of-the-box idea of Business One. The thought of rolling out SAP to a manufacturing plant in only 2 months was unheard of. In fact, back then only about 20% of companies that implemented SAP actually shipped product on the day they went live. I am proud to say we were one of them.

It had already been a long day. I started at 7AM the morning before go-live. We were extracting, validating, loading and re-validating the open data up until nearly midnight. Then we decided to go to Denny's for dinner / breakfast because we were starving by the time we had finished validating the data. We had scheduled the Receiving Department to come in at 2:30AM to start receiving components that were piling up on our receiving dock since the cut-off of our legacy system (the previous Friday). After helping the Receiving Department process goods receipts on our new SAP system for a couple of hours I was thinking about going home to take a shower and get a little sleep. But before I knew it, it was 6AM and the customer service team came in to support the East Coast customers. Their first question was, "How do I log in again? I know we were trained but I forgot." I ended up supporting our users throughout the day and finally went home at about 9PM that night. It was the longest work day of my life (about 38 hours), but it is one of my most proud and memorable efforts as well.

As many things in life, much is developed out of necessity. I developed this 2 month approach to rolling out SAP because I had a very demanding management team and SMART is a very dynamic company. We always had too much to do in a very short amount of time. However, the advantage of having a very demanding management team was that I had their full support. That is a key ingredient to the recipe of a successful implementation. The executive management team realized the impact that an ERP implementation has on an organization. Implementations such as these require decisions to be made quickly. The management team must include employees on the project that they trust to make good business process decisions. They must empower the team members to develop the "To-Be" business processes. The management team also must provide the project managers with the resources to complete a project successfully. Details of the project team resources will be covered in Chapter 3 "The Project Preparation".

Another key ingredient to a successful 2 month SAP implementation is to use a "cookie-cutter" approach. Start with business process configuration that already exists and extend that configuration to the new site or manufacturing plant. There is much debate over this approach but it is the author's opinion that it is not only possible, but it is the right thing to do for your company. There are several pros and cons to this approach, but throughout this book, you will see that there are many more pros than cons.

Most people's knee-jerk reaction is to say, "But our company is different than other companies." One could go as far as to say that it is the difference between companies that give them a competitive advantage in their respective markets. I agree completely. I am the first to admit that no two plants are the same within a company let alone the fact that no to companies are the same.

A company's ERP system is not what defines them. It is not what creates a company's culture. It is not what gives their products special features. It does not make a company's design engineers better than another's. It is not what makes one company's manufacturing process better than another's. It does not give them better customer service or even better supply chain partners. It is people who do all of that. Managers and employees of a company differentiate a company amongst its competitors.

Companies that are well-organized are better positioned for competition. Well-organized companies do not have extra layers of fat. They run leaner than their competitors. They try their best to standardize business processes across all sites. Well-organized companies speak the same language as it relates to their industry, their business processes and their applications. They can quickly transfer materials or human resources to other plants to accommodate changes in market conditions. Well-organized companies are flexible and they can respond quickly to customer's requests. Each site acts as part of the whole instead of an entirely different entity. Well-organized companies have the tools to manage their business well.

I have worked in companies that were so large that one hand did not know what the other was doing. It is very frustrating dealing with companies like this. As the customer, you often find yourself as the communication venue that notifies one part of a company about what another part of their company is doing. A well-managed business has a single face to the customer.

Imagine a company that runs the same business processes in each of their facilities. They use a single instance of SAP that allows every employee in the world access to the same set of information (restricted by their security roles of course). They can see inventory in all of the plants. They can move manufacturing of a particular product to which ever plant makes the most sense. When employees talk about inventory in stock location 00, regardless of the plant they are in, everyone knows they are talking about inventory that is in "Put-Away" (on the cart on its way from receiving to the raw materials stock room). When an employee in one plant talks about MD04, everyone knows they are talking about supply and demand. It doesn't matter what products or services each company or plant offers, everyone in the company speaks the same language. It allows employees in one plant to help employees in another plant very easily. It allows the same message to be delivered to a customer or supplier. This company is the most competitive in its market because it can keep costs low and inventory turns high. Because there is a single instance of their applications, they have a smaller IT staff and they can centralize many of their functions. This is a well-run company. I am not describing an unattainable utopia. I am describing the company that I worked for; the company that I helped to build while in my meager roll as an IT professional.

The fact is that no matter what products or services a manufacturing company offers to their customer base, there are core business processes that are standard. The order-to-cash process and the procure-to-pay process are basically the same across almost all businesses. This is where an ERP's strengths are. An ERP like SAP is designed to run core business processes for a company to receive orders from customers, provide materials and / or services, to invoice customers and receive payments. It is designed to process purchase orders, receive inventory and process payments to suppliers. This is not rocket science. These are core business processes which are common amongst almost all companies that exist to make a profit. The fact that these core business processes are the same for most profit-oriented companies makes it possible to use a cookie-cutter approach to implement SAP. I know because I have done it more than 10 times for a variety of companies. This experience has made me a believer in the concept of utilizing pre-configured systems. In essence, we had created a system and used it as a pre-configured system to implement SAP for subsequent acquisitions.

Chapter 2
The SMART Approach

"Leaders need to be optimists. Their vision is beyond the present."
– Rudy Guiliani

I first documented the SMART approach to implementing SAP several years ago when I was preparing for an implementation at one of Solectron Corporation's manufacturing plants in Puerto Rico. I wanted to give their management team an idea what they were about to get into. I also used it as a means to communicate tips and tricks they could use to get a jump start on some of the activities that need to be performed during the project. I coined it, The SMART Approach to implementing SAP. SMART is an acronym for "Standard Migration and Application Roll-out Technique". That went over well because the name of the company that I worked for was SMART Modular Technologies and "SMART" was an acronym for "Surface Mount And Reflow Technologies".

SMART had been acquired by Solectron Corporation and Solectron's manufacturing plant in Puerto Rico was placed within our newly-created division.

The SMART Approach begins with sending a packet of files to the management team of the site that is about to undergo an SAP implementation. The packet includes an overview document that outlines the approach and explains the packet contents. The overview document itself is like a

"What To Expect When You Are Expecting" type of document. It outlines the objectives of the project. It talks about the business process mapping and it gives the readers an overview of the company's SAP landscape. From a high level, it describes what is involved in configuring the system and the activities involved in the data migration. It outlines the project team responsibilities and stresses the importance of key users and champions. The document also outlines the cut-over and post-go-live support. Finally it outlines their deliverables to us, the project team.

This document is an important part of an implementation project. Ideally it would be sent to all of the managers of the migrating plant, but at a minimum should be sent to the Site Controller and the General Manager of the plant.

The SMART Approach packet contains the following documents:

- System Integration Questionnaire
- Currency Questionnaire
- Corporate Chart of Accounts
- Data Migration Templates
- Sample Contact List
- Sample User Authorization Template
- Sample Project Plan
- Sample Issues Log
- Sample Cut-over Plan
- Sample Post Go-Live Issues Log
- Sample Integration Test Scenarios
- Sample Integration Test Schedule

System Integration Questionnaire

The configuration questionnaire (figure 2.0) is a set of questions posed by the SAP Business Systems Analysts (BSAs). It contains some general questions plus it has sections specific to each of the SAP modules - Finance (FI), Sales and Distribution (SD), and Materials Management (MM) / Production Planning (PP), etc. I suggest customizing this questionnaire to fit your business requirements.

Figure 2.0 Sample System Integration Questionnaire

System Integration Questionnaire

1) What application(s) and versions does your company currently use for business transactions and reporting?
2) Who supports these systems/applications for you now?
3) How many people currently use this system at your site?
4) How many of them only access the system for information, but do not actually transact on the system themselves.
5) What makes & models of printers do you use? What printers are used in which departments and to print which documents?
6) What is your physical address and mailing address?

Sales and Distribution

1) How many active customers are in the ERP and Financial systems?
2) Are credit limits used in your ERP or Financial system?
3) What credit management tools are used?
4) How many sales employees does the company employ?
5) How many sales representative firms are used?
6) How many sales orders are on the backlog?
7) Do you print and send sales order acknowledgements? If so, please provide an example.
8) How is pricing maintained? (i.e. On price lists in the system or manually in the sales order?)
9) Is an automated material availability check used? If so, what is it based on?
10) Is Customer or Vendor Consignment used?
11) Is customer EDI used? If so, how many customers transact via EDI? How many EDI transactions are processed daily?
12) What freight carriers are used?
13) How many shipping terminals are used in the ERP system?
14) What are your shipping system solutions?
15) What is the shipment volume on a daily basis?
16) Are outer box label printers used? If so, what are the customer requirements?
17) Are barcodes required for any documents? If so, what are they?
18) How are RMA's (Return Material Authorizations) handled?
19) Please provide examples of any reports used for Sales/Customer Service, Shipping, RMA and Accounts Receivable.

Figure 2.0 Sample System Integration Questionnaire (cont'd)

Finance

1) Is this business a separate legal entity (separate company) or is it a product line that is being purchased and absorbed into the company?
2) Will this business have its own Finance department or is this being handled by the existing Corporate Finance personnel?
3) How many Product Lines does your company have and what are they? (i.e. Memory, Flash, Flat Panel Displays, etc.)
4) Are assets handled in your ERP System?

Materials Management / Production Planning

1) How many vendors are set up in the ERP?
2) How many active materials (part numbers) are there?
3) What is the nomenclature of your part numbers?
4) How many active BOMs (Bills of Materials) are there? Are they single level or multi-level?
5) How many open purchase orders are in the ERP?
6) Do you have an approved vendors list? If so, where is it maintained and by whom? How many records are maintained?
7) How are MRO items handled?
8) How many storage locations are there?
9) Have we acquired any inventory? If so, how much of each part number?
10) Is vendor consigned inventory used?
11) Is vendor EDI used? If so, for how many vendors and how many transactions are run daily?
12) Please provide examples of your Purchase Order forms, Production Pick Lists, Work Orders, and Goods Receipt Documents.

Currency Determination

The currency guideline is designed to help determine the appropriate functional currency to configure for the new Company Code in SAP. The Functional Currency is the currency of the primary economic environment in which the entity operates; normally, that is, the currency of the environment in which an entity primarily generate and expends cash. It is not necessarily the local transactional currency. Transactions such as purchase orders and sales orders can be performed in many different currencies which are determine by the location of your suppliers and customers and your agreements with them. It is also not necessarily the Group Currency which is used for financial consolidation and corporate reporting. The table in Figure 2.1 provides a guideline to help determine whether to use the local currency or the corporate currency as the functional currency for your new company code in SAP. In this example the corporate currency is USD.

Figure 2.1 Guidelines for Functional Currency Determination

Determination of Functional Currency		
Indicator	Indication of the *local* currency as the functional currency	Indication of the *corporate* currency (USD) as the functional currency
Cash Flows	Mainly in the local currency and does not affect parent's cash flows.	Directly impacts the parent's current cash flows and is readily available for remittance to the parent.
Sales Prices	Mainly determined by local competition and local government regulation.	Responsive on a short-term basis to changes in exchange rates such as worldwide competition or by international prices.
Sales Market	Active local sales market for the entity products.	Most sales are in the U.S. or are denominated in US Dollars.
Expenses	Mainly determined by local conditions.	Production and materials are mainly obtained through U.S. sources.
Financing	Primarily in the local currency and serviced by funds generated by the entity operations.	Significant US Dollar financing or reliance on the U.S. parent to service debt obligations.
Intercompany transactions and arrangements	Few intercompany transactions with the parent.	Frequent and extensive intercompany transactions with the parent, or the entity is an investment or financing device for the parent.

Another way to determine the proper functional currency is to use the Functional Currency Questionnaire. The Functional currency questionnaire provides more than a guideline. Once the questions are answered, it makes the proper functional currency obvious. It will show what functional currency the new company code should be configured with. Figure 2.3 shows a sample of the functional currency questionnaire. The following is an excerpt from the SMART Approach document:

"It is also necessary to determine the operational currency that your business will use within SAP. The currency decision is based on a set of criteria that we obtain from the Currency Questionnaire."

Please fill out the currency questionnaire. We have enclosed a copy of this questionnaire for your convenience. This should be done early in the process.

Figure 2.3 Sample Functional Currency Questionnaire

QUESTIONNAIR TO DETERMINE THE FUNCTIONAL CURRENCY OF A FOREIGN SUBSIDIARIE OR BRANCH				
1. Name of the Entity: (To be completed by the Corporate Finance)		2. Questionnaire Completed by:		
3. Functional Currency Determination: Approved by:		4. Date:		
Controller's Office:				
Treasury:				
Tax:				
5. What is the primary currency for General Ledger for the Operation?				
PLEASE INDICATE ANSWERS IN (%) FOR QUESTIONS 5-10		OTHER CURRENCIES Example:		
(Please indicate which currency followed by %)		USD %	GPB %	EUR %
		48%	50%	2%
6. The national currency of the country in which the entity is a resident. (e.g. country of incorporation for legal entity or country in which branch locates)				
7. The currencies of the entity's cash flow from Revenue				
8. The currencies of the entity's cash flow from Expense				
9. The currencies which the entity borrows from and/or invests in Externally				
10. The currencies which the entity borrows from and/or invests in Internally (Intercompany)				
11. The currencies of total cash flow, including operating and financing cash flow				
12. Sales market and pricing – are the competitors mostly locally based or internationally based? Are product/service pricing responsive to exchange rate changes, or determined by local conditions with little regard to exchange rate changes?				
13. Sourcing market and pricing – are vendors mostly locally based or internationally based? Are product/service pricing responsive to exchange rate changes, or determined by local conditions with little regard to exchange rate changes?				

Corporate Chart of Accounts

The Corporate Chart of Accounts (COA) is included in the SMART Approach packet because the newly acquired company will need to map their COA to the Corporate COA. The Corporate COA is already configured in SAP system and used by the rest of the company. It is required that the new company must migrate to the company's standard corporate chart of accounts. The following is an excerpt from the SMART Approach document:

"A critical piece of the integration is the mapping of the general ledger. The first step in achieving synergies throughout all of our sites is using a single or common COA (Chart of Accounts). This obviously makes it easy for financial reporting to Corporate."

Another thing you can do to get a jumpstart on this conversion is to map your COA to the Corporate COA. We have enclosed a copy of the Corporate COA for your convenience. This will need to be done early on in the process.

Data Migration Templates

Data migration templates are used to map data from the legacy systems to SAP. These templates detail each field that needs to be extracted from the legacy system and loaded into SAP. They specify how field values from the legacy system need to be translated to new values in SAP. They also state what default values may need to be loaded into SAP. Data migration templates are used for objects such as customer master records, vendor master records, material master records, bill of materials (BOMs), purchase orders, sale orders, etc. The following is an excerpt from the SMART Approach document:

"Data Migration is simply moving data from a legacy system to the new system. We load data into SAP using a combination of LSMW and BDC programs. LSMW (Legacy System Migration Warehouse) is a SAP standard tool used to load data into SAP tables. BDC (Batch Data Communication) programs are used to load data into SAP by emulating transactions.

One of the most important parts of data migration is getting the data out of your system (the legacy system). To assist you in this process we have provided some templates in MS Excel® that specify the fields that we need for each data object. A data object is a set of data such as customer masters, vendor masters, or sales orders. There are master data objects and open data objects. Master data is fairly stagnant. It includes information on customers, vendors, materials (part numbers) BOMs, etc. Open data is transactional data including information on sales orders, purchase orders, G/L balances, inventory balances, etc. Open data changes much more frequently than master data.

Please review the templates that we have included in this package. Please consider the data that we will be loading into SAP to make sure that it includes the information you will need for your business. We have determined that the fields in these templates will give us enough information to perform the basic transactions in SAP."

You can get a jumpstart on the conversion by beginning to extract the data outlined in the data migration templates.

Sample Contact List

Another document included in the SMART Approach package is a contact list. But this is not a simple list of project contacts. It is much more. It is actually a "Buddy List". In this cookie-cutter approach, we partner key people from the newly acquired site to their counterpart in a nearby plant. "Nearby" is a relative term considering that the company has plants spread around the world. We create a sister site scenario where the sister site is in the closest time zone and/or has people that speak the same language.

In this book, I will refer to key people from the newly acquired site as "Key Users". Their counterparts in a site already on SAP will be referred to in this book as "Champions".

There should be business process champions in each of the major facilities. These champions are representatives from different departments throughout the company. They know their jobs very well – better than anyone else in the department, and they are the go-to people within their respective departments when peers have questions on SAP transactions or business processes.

The buddy list partners the champions from the sister site with their key user counterparts in the newly acquired site. The buddy list also contains the names of these people's managers and their respective phone numbers and email addresses. I will discuss more about the champions and the buddy list in Chapter 3 "The Project Preparation".

Sample User Authorization Template

User Authorizations in public companies have changed dramatically over the years as a result of the Segregation of Duties (SOD) requirements in section 404 of the Sarbanes-Oxley Act (SOX). Before SOX, we simply used to copy one user with reference to another. This would copy all of the profiles and SAP roles to the new user. Therefore, the User Authorization Template was simply a map showing all of the people in the newly acquired company with their names and their titles mapped to people in the sister site.

Now with SOX, we still use this template, but it is used as a guideline and not used to actually map users' access directly in SAP. I recommend using SAP's Access Enforcer and Compliance Calibrator now known as SAP Access Controls within the SAP GRC® (Governance, Risk and Compliance) suite to maintain segregation of duties compliance. The BSAs use the User Authorization Template as a guideline, when they map all of the new users to the SAP roles that will be assigned to them in Access Controls.

Sample Project Plan

This is fairly self-explanatory. The SMART Approach package should include a sample of the 2 month implementation project plan. This simply gives the management team an idea of the tasks involved in an SAP implementation project. I suggest saving the MS Project file in a .pdf format so the recipient does not need MS project to view the project plan. We will dive into the project plan in Chapter 6 "The Detailed Project Plan".

Sample Issues Log

A sample of an issues log is included in the SMART Approach package. This gives them very good examples of the types of issues that come up during a project and how they are resolved. The issues log is a log of the detailed issues that come up during the project. All kinds of issues are logged. Business Process issues, data mapping issues, printer issues, desktop GUI issues, etc. All issues are logged, assigned an owner, and a due date. The issues are classified by criticality. Some issues are not on the critical path. It is important to know which issues need to be resolved prior to go-live and which ones can wait until afterwards. Some can wait until after go-live, but may need to be resolved prior to the first month-end financial closing. The issues log is a key component of a 2 month implementation.

Sample Cut-Over Plan

The package also includes a sample cut-over plan. This is extremely good information to share with a company that is about to undergo an SAP implementation. It gives them a very good idea of the go-live activities day-by-day and hour-by-hour. By reviewing a sample of the cut-over plan, they can see the amount of down-time they should expect during the cut-over weekend.

Sample Post Go-Live Issues Log

By sharing a sample of a post go-live issues log in the SMART Approach packet, the company that is about to undergo an SAP implementation will have an idea of what problems may occur during and just after the go-live of an implementation.

Much like the Issues Log mentioned above, the Post Go-Live Issues Log is a means of logging and tracking the progress of problem resolution. But the post go-live issues log begins at the time of go-live. Issues are classified by the impact they have on the company's ability to conduct business. The highest priority is given to "production down" situations; the lowest priority is given to "nice to have" features.

Production down situations are conditions that prevent the company from being able perform business critical system transactions. Examples of these transactions include: the ability to enter a sales order, ship products, invoice customers, the ability to process payments from customers, production order processing, purchasing, and paying vendors.

These must be fixed immediately. If the implementation is done properly, production down situations do not exist.

The rule of thumb is that if a user brings up a problem that cannot be resolved by simply showing them the correct way to process a transaction (on-the-job training), then it should be logged on the post go-live issues log. Another rule of thumb is that no items should be added to the post go-live issues log after the site has been live on SAP for two weeks. Issues that are brought up after two weeks of conducting business on SAP should be logged using your company's normal IT support process.

It is a best practice to review the post go-live issues log after the project is complete. It allows us to learn from our past mistakes and improve the next project. Some items may be added to the project plan or cut-over plan for the next project as a result of these lessons learned and as a preventative measure for the next project.

Sample Integration Test Scenarios

Integration test scenarios are sometimes easy to talk about but difficult to visualize in enough detail to be meaningful. By including sample integration test scenarios in the packet, people will have a better understanding of the level of detail that we will need to test. The users from the newly acquired business will be involved in process of creating these integration test scenarios for their implementation. With the SMART Approach, the integration test scenarios are designed to meet the needs of most manufacturing companies, but need to be reviewed and agreed upon by the key users and champions.

Sample Integration Test Schedule

A sample of the integration test schedule will show those involved the level of participation we will need from the user community. At the same time, it gives them a sense of the tight schedule they will be under. It is a good time to remind them that they should not plan vacation time during integration testing.

The SMART Approach package is a very important part of an SAP implementation. Communication is the most important part of a project. This package is the beginning of this communication. It is designed to prepare the new site for the project ahead. It will prepare them for the kick-off presentation which is the next extremely important means of communication.

When learning to write a speech, you are instructed to begin by telling the audience what you plan to tell them. In the body of the presentation, you tell them what you want them to know. Then you should wrap up the presentation by summarizing what you told them. To compare this to project communication, the SMART Approach package is the introduction where you tell them what you plan to tell them. The kick-off presentation is the body, where you tell them what they need to know. You will spend the rest of the project communicating the summary, where you remind them over and over what you told them in the kick-off meeting. ☺

Chapter 3
Project Preparation

"Doing is a quantum leap from imagining. Thinking about swimming isn't much like actually getting in the water. Actually getting in the water can take your breath away. The defense force inside of us wants us to be cautious, to stay away from anything as intense as a new kind of action. Its job is to protect us, and it categorically avoids anything resembling danger. But it's often wrong. Anything worth doing is worth doing too soon."

– Barbara Sher

By using the "cookie-cutter" approach to rolling out SAP, the project preparation phase of the project is greatly reduced. Templates for the documentation will already exist. You literally begin with documents that were used in the previous implementations. In this chapter, I will discuss the most important components to consider when preparing for a 2 month implementation. To begin with, let's talk about the team.

The Project Team

Overall there are four main groups of people that compose the project team. One group is the Project Sponsors which include the executives from Corporate as well as the the senior management team at the new site. Another group is the SAP Team comprised of people from the IT department and /

or a SAP consulting partner and project manager(s). The key users from the newly acquired site is the third group; and the fourth is the champions from the sister site.

The team members selected for the project make all the difference in the world. Literally, the individuals on the project are the most important factor for success or failure. The acquisition and integration of a company should be the most important project in the company at that time. Therefore, you should put your best people on this project. Because this is only a 2 month project, you can afford to put your best people on the project. In fact, you can't afford not to. Not only should you put your best SAP team members on the project, you should also put your best team leads from each of your departments on the project from both the newly acquired company *and* its sister site.

The Project Sponsors

It is absolutely critical to have executive sponsorship of an SAP implementation. The corporate executives such as the CEO, CFO, and COO must support the project. They must also support the approach and back up the project team if / when managers from the new site escalate concerns about the approach. This is usually not a problem because the executive team understands value of running the same business processes worldwide. The site managers in turn need to embrace this approach and trust the project team to what is best for the company and support any issues that may arise. Company politics can quickly derail the project, but when the employees see that the management team agrees with the approach, they will be much more cooperative.

It is my experience that executive support grows over time. Executive support is something that must be earned. But once you have proved that the approach works in your organization, the trust grows rapidly, which makes the project run smoothly.

The SAP Team

Many people will be surprised to hear this, but it is the belief of the author that the SAP team should be very small. As stated earlier, I have had much experience rolling out SAP. I have also had the luxury of learning from other's mistakes. Many of the companies that have a bad experience implementing SAP have had huge SAP teams. The reality is that SAP is very configurable and there are several ways the system can be configured to meet the objective of a given business process. I was once explaining a business problem relating to RMAs (Return Material Authorizations) to a SAP SD (Sales and Distribution) consultant. He said, "I can think of five ways to resolve this in SAP. Let's talk about three of them."

People have different experiences, different ideas, and different comfort areas. When there are several people on a project who are responsible for the same SAP module, much time is wasted debating the best way to achieve the desired business process outcome.

It is difficult enough to get agreement between the different modules, let alone within the same module. In a 2 month implementation, there is little time for this debate. The bickering that will come from having too many cooks in the kitchen will also bring down the moral of the team. The moral of the team is extremely important. Maintaining a high team morale results in a much more productive team.

Figure 3.1 shows the composition of the IT Applications team that I use in the SMART Approach to rolling out SAP ECC and BI (Business Intelligence). It outlines the team members' responsibilities and their level of participation in the project. Notice that there are only six full-time resources including the project manager, three modular BSAs, and a technical resource. There is one full-time resource from the new company who is responsible for data extraction from the legacy system. There are two part-time resources (one for Basis and Security, and one for Business Intelligence reporting tool configuration).

This small team is all that is required from IT

Applications for a successful SAP ECC implementation using the SMART Approach no matter how large the new site is. I have used a smaller team in SAP implementations at sites with less than 350 people, but regardless of the size of the new company, the ideal team is represented in Figure 3.1.

In situations where you need to rollout SAP to multiple sites simultaneously, the organizational configuration for the all sites should be done at the same time for all sites by a single team. However, during the rest of the project, I recommend having a team for each manufacturing site / distribution center where the full-time resources are dedicated to the site, and the part-time resources can be shared by multiple sites. (Note: In this scenario, it is also wise to add a prefix to the descriptions of the site-specific transports that denote the site that the configuration is for. In addition, I would recommend a senior project manager over all of the site implementations to help coordinate timings of activities between sites, but if necessary each team's project manager can work together to accomplish this.

If you are implementing SAP in a big bang approach to many sites across a large geography, I would recommend a different approach. If for example, you need to roll out SAP to 150 stores throughout the country and they all had to go live at the same time, the implementation approach and deployment strategy would need to be more centralized. The SMART Approach would not be a good solution for that type of scenario. However, many of the sample documents and concepts outlined in this book apply to all SAP implementations.

Figure 3.1 outlines the ideal team for the SMART Approach to implementing SAP ECC and BI. If your organization has already implemented other enterprise applications such as CRM, SRM, APO, HR, etc., you would obviously need people to cover these applications. It is a good practice to have a cross-trained team that can handle multiple applications, but there is a limit to how many applications or modules, one person can handle during a fast implementation.

If at all possible, I recommend using internal team members for the BSA and data migration positions on the team. By "internal" team members, I mean employees of the parent company or long-term contractors who are familiar with the configuration, processes, and data that are used by the parent company.

The project manager should be experienced in fast SAP implementations. They need this experience to lead the rest of the team and keep them focused on the priorities and the critical path.

Figure 3.1 IT Applications team for the SMART Approach.

Position	Responsibilities	Participation
Project Manager	Prepare and maintain the project budget, project plan, cut-over plan, issues log, post go-live issues log, travel plan, and assembly of the project documentation.	Full-Time
FI/CO BSA	Work with the business to validate that the "AS-IS" processes can be migrated to the standard To-Be processes and work to fill any gaps. Document the business process gaps and the configuration approach in the Blueprint document.	Full-Time
SD (CS/LE) BSA	Configure and document the configuration of the new site in SAP. Test the configuration in DEV & QA. Prepare the transport list. Prepare the data migration templates. Work with the key users, champions, and Data Migration expert on the data files for loading into SAP. Work with the champions to prepare the Integration Test Scenarios. Assist the key users and champions by answering questions and resolving issues uncovered during Integration Testing and UAT. Assist the champions in training the key users and the rest of the users in the new site. Support the cut-over activities leading up to and including the go-live. Provide post go-live support to the new site.	
MM/PP/QM BSA		
ABAP / LSMW	Maintain Smart Form additions, report modifications, and system integration points. Prepare and load the data files in SAP.	Full-Time
Legacy System Expert	Extract data from legacy system and prepare data load files. Work with key users, champions, BSAs and LSMW resource to ensure extracted data is valid. (This person is usually from the new site and rarely familiar with SAP.)	Full-Time
Basis & Security	Maintain SAP security, and transport requests. Communicate with the infrastructure team to ensure SAP compatibility and connectivity with desktop PCs, printers, and the network.	Part-Time
BW / BI BSA	Maintain the master data objects and process chains for reporting in BI.	Part-Time

The Key Users

In this book, "Key Users" is the term we use to identify key people within each department at the site that is undergoing an SAP implementation. There is a key user from each department that will perform transactions in SAP. If a department does not use the legacy system, it is unlikely that they will need to devote a key user to the project.

Key users play an absolutely critical role in the implementation and they are a vital part of the implementation team. They are the people who communicate the "AS-IS" processes to the SAP team. They are the ones who review the standard corporate processes and help determine if those processes will work in their line of business. They are trained on SAP during the user test phase and actually perform the integration / user acceptance testing in the QA systems. If there are problems with the testing, they communicate this to the champions and the SAP team who will resolve the problem. The key users work with the champions and the SAP team mapping the data from the legacy system to SAP at a very detailed level (field by field). They are involved in validating the data that is extracted from the legacy system. They approve the data to be loaded in the SAP system. They also validate the data after it has been loaded and give their approval that the data is correct.

These are the people that know their business processes the best. They will be responsible for the new business processes using SAP transactions. By the end of the project, they will have more knowledge on SAP than anyone else in their department. To some extent, they will help train others in their department and become the go-to person in their department for questions on processes and on SAP. They are the champions of the future, who someday could help implement SAP at another site.

It should now be obvious that these people are hands-on. They should be the "go-to" people of their departments already. Some companies make the mistake of assigning hands-off managers to the project team. They do this because the company believes that those managers are responsible for the business processes. The people that should be on the project should be the people who are doing the job today. These people should be empowered to make decisions during the project. They can be managers or supervisors, but they must be hands-on. Companies also make the mistake of assigning new employees to the project team. They do this because they believe the tenured employees need to run the business until the cut-over. This causes a two-fold problem. First, the new employees do not know the business well enough to raise a red flag if the new process will not accommodate a certain variation or customer-specific requirement. Second, the tenured employees will not know SAP well enough when the system goes live to play the role of the "go-to person" in their department. Upon go live, suddenly the new employee who now knows how the processes run in SAP will be the most important person in the department. They will become the go-to person by default.

The Champions

In this book, "Champion" is the term we use to identify the business process experts from the parent company who works in the trenches every day. They use SAP every day to process the business transactions. They know the business better than anyone else in their department and they know how the company uses SAP transactions to get the job done.

During the implementation of SAP at a new site, these champions are responsible for training the key users at the new site. They train them not only on SAP transactions but also on the business processes that are running in the rest of the sites. They work side-by-side with the key users during the data migration preparation and during the integration testing. The project budget should include travel expenses for these champions to work at the new site side-by-side with the key users. The champions are the glue that holds the new site together as key users start to come unraveled when the magnitude of the project relative to the timeline hits them. The key users lean on the champions during and after the project.

The Buddy System

One of the vital ingredients of a successful implementation following the SMART Approach is the buddy system. We pair up the key users with the champions who perform the same job function. For example, we introduce the key user in Customer Service at the site undergoing the SAP implementation to the Customer Service champion from the sister site that is already on SAP.

Likewise we pair up the key user in Purchasing with the champion in Purchasing and the key user in Planning with the champion in Planning. One of the forms the site should send back from the preparation package is the buddy list including the key users and their managers.

Even though you receive this list of key users from the site, it is important to contact each manager of the key users to get their support. They need to support the involvement of their employees on the project. The project will consume much of these people's lives over the next couple of months so it is important that their manager does not change their focus during the project. Figure 3.2 shows a portion of a buddy list where "Adtron Phoenix" represents the new site about to implement SAP and "SMART Fremont" represents the sister site that is already on SAP.

Figure 3.2 Sample Buddy List

| ADTRON Phoenix - (602) 735- | | | | SMART Fremont - (510) | | Project |
KEY USER NAME / MANAGER'S NAME	MODULE	AREA OF RESPONSIBILITY	CHAMPION NAME	MANAGER'S NAME		BSA
Denise / Gloria 602-735- gloria	FI	Cost Accounting, G/L	Ryan x8782 ryan	Colleen x8208 colleen		Jing x5369 jing
Denise / Gloria 602-735- gloria	FI	Accounts Payable (A/P)	Delia x5390 delia	Colleen x8208 colleen		Jing x5369 jing
Michelle / Gloria 602-735- michelle	FI	Accounts Receivable (A/R), Fixed Assets	Veronica x8250 veronica	Lee x8534 lee		Jing x5369 jing
Liz / Jamie 602-735- liz	MM	Warehousing and Inv Control, Stockroom	Gopal x8554 gopal	Ashok x8109 ashok		Anil x5376 anil
Bill / Jamie 602-735- william	MM	Inventory Purchasing and MRO Purchasing	Jennifer x8237 jennifer	Anjali x8109 anjali		Anil x5376 anil
Liz / Jamie 602-735- liz	MM	Receiving	Gopal x8554 gopal	Ashok x8129 ashok		Anil x5376 anil
Liz / Jamie 602-735- liz	PP	Production Control and Manufacturing	Bryan x8537 bryan	Bobby x8154 bobb		Anil x5376 anil
Liz / Jamie 602-735- liz	PP	Master Scheduling	Bryan x8537 bryan	Bobby x8154 bobb		Anil x5376 anil
Bonnie / Bobby 602-735- bob	PP	Document Control	Louis x8169 louis	Saty x8561 saty		Anil x5376 anil

These "buddies" learn a lot from each other. The key users learn the corporate business processes and procedures from the champions. They learn the how to perform the business transactions in SAP. They learn which reports are already in place to satisfy their data mining and analytics needs. They learn where to go on the corporate intranet portal to find the documentation and forms that they will need. They learn how intertwined the SAP business process are and who to talk to in other departments as business processes span across multiple business areas. They learn the culture and language of the company.

The champions learn the business processes within the new site and how to relate them to the business processes endorsed by Corporate. By teaching, they learn SAP better and the underlying requirements of the configuration and master data. The champions lean on the SAP team when they come across business process issues that they have not encountered before. This in turn helps them become more efficient in their jobs when they return home.

A crucial role that the buddy system plays in the project is that of support, both during *and* after the project. During the project the champions support the key users and help train all of the users in the new site as I have mentioned above. Because they know the job better than anyone else, and because they answer the key user's questions throughout the project, they become the obvious choice for the key users to continue to call if they have problems or questions in the future. Upon completion of the project, when the champions have returned home, if the key users encounter issues, their first call is to their buddy in their sister plant. Only if the champion does not know the answer, the SAP Business Systems Analysts gets involved.

This process is crucial to running an efficient organization. The reason for the key user to call their champion buddy first is the same reason the other people in the department lean on the champion before calling IT. The SAP Team is busy working on strategic projects and new site implementations. They are also paid very well compared to key users and champions. So, if someone else in the company can answer the question, it is more efficient and cost effective to let them do so. The more questions that are posed to the champions, the more they learn and the more self-sufficient they become. This is especially crucial in an outsourced IT environment, but applies to an internal SAP team in the same way.

The Champion Community

Upon completion of the project, the key users become members of the Champion Community. The Champion Community is like a software users' group. It consists of all of the champions from all of the departments in all of the company's locations around the world. The Champion Community should meet twice per quarter or at least twice in a six month period.

One meeting is a site meeting. This is a meeting of all of the champions within a company location or campus and at least one SAP BSA (ideally one BSA from each SAP module or component). The champions all represent different departments. In these meetings, they review issues they have with SAP and business processes that span over multiple departments. They are looking for efficiencies across all departments. There is a round table discussion in each of these meetings that allow the champions to bring up ideas or talk about concerns on any business topic. This meeting provides an opportunity for department representatives to bond. In many companies there is a little animosity between departments. The Champion Community is a way to help break down department walls and rid the company of this animosity. If none of the champions step up to organize this, it can be led by a site SAP manager or SAP lead. But it is best led by one of the champions. The community can hold elections and select a coordinator if they choose to do so.

Another activity that happens during these site-based Champion Community meetings is training. This is a perfect opportunity to perform mini SAP training sessions for the

Champions. Unless intentionally scheduled for a topic that will take longer, the training portion of the meeting should only last about a half hour. An agenda item at each meeting is to decide what training subject will be covered in the next meeting. Because the attendees of this meeting represent many different departments, the training is fundamental in nature. Training topics would include SAP navigation, search functionality, and tips & tricks that would help all SAP users.

The second meeting is a global meeting. This is not a meeting with all champions worldwide. Actually, it is a set of meetings for champions within the same departments, but with their counterparts at different sites. In these meetings, each champion shares issues or business problems that they have encountered at their site. Often they find people at other sites have encounter the same issue and can share how the problem was resolved.

These global department Champion Community meetings can also include training via a screen sharing application. Because the attendees are all from the same department, it is a good opportunity to offer detailed training specific to the transactions that are used in the respective departments.

In these global department meetings the champions share information they learned in the site meetings about inter-department processes; and in the site meetings they share information they learned in the global department meetings if applicable.

The global meetings continue the process of our constant endeavor to maintain the same business processes and best practices across all company locations. Maintaining the same business processes across all sites allows IT departments to stay lean and it attributes to the success of the fast implementation approach to add new sites. It's like the circle of life. Each component feeds into another, creating synergies that result in continuous improvement for not only world-class but best-in-class organizations.

The War Room

A war room is a room in which the project team works during the project at the site that is undergoing the ERP implementation. The room should be large enough to hold the project team members and key users that will be performing testing. The room should have at least one dry erase board and unless a wireless network is available it should have plenty of network connections - at least one for each of the SAP team member and one for each of the business champions that they will be working with at any one time. The room should also have a printer and 4 – 6 PCs as needed for the people without laptop computers.

The Training Room

A training room should also be set up at the site depending on the size of the site and the number of the people that need to be trained. This room should contain at least one dry-erase board, a projector and screen, and at least one PC for every 2 people (ideally 1 PC per person). It should be sized to hold the people of the largest department that needs to be trained. Usually training is held for one department at a time. If necessary you can split up a department into multiple training sessions, but the training schedule will need to be considered. There are only 2 weeks of training and every potential SAP user at the site needs to be trained.

The High Level Project Plan

How do you go about building a project plan for an implementation cycle that most people think is impossible? What I am about to share with you is considered somewhat unconventional and many project managers would roll their eyes and quickly discard the idea. But I have used it many times and it has shown undeniable results.

The first thing I do when I am informed of a pending acquisition is obtain a calendar that I can mark up. In fact, I start by reviewing an old project calendar - one that I have used before to plan prior implementations. I use it as a reference to ensure that I allocate roughly the same amount of time for the activities that I have accomplished before. I then compare it to a new calendar. On the new calendar, I look at the next few months and make sure that all holidays and work-related days off are represented on the calendar.

By the way, just because the calendar shows holidays and work days off, it doesn't mean that my team or I will necessarily be able to take them off. But what it does show me is the challenges I will face with the rest of the company's employees, key users, and champions. When implementing SAP at a plant in a different country, make sure you contact the site and find out when they have scheduled time off. Also, it is critical to note your company's fiscal month ends. Go-Live is always over a fiscal month end and the Finance department will always be short-staffed during the two fiscal month ends that will occur during the project. When planning an implementation it is wise to avoid going live on fiscal year ends and even at the end of fiscal quarters.

Many companies have seasonal busy times. It is important to understand the peaks and valleys of the company's busy times. It is best to plan your go-live in the slowest quarter. In fact, for most companies the best time to plan a go-live is at the beginning of the second month of the slowest fiscal quarter. Unfortunately I was rarely afforded this luxury. Growing companies always have projects that cannot wait for the ideal fiscal month for the go-live because there are other projects in the pipeline.

The Starting Line

To accomplish any objective, one should start with the end in mind. Therefore, I start by selecting the tentative Go-

Live date. As a rule of thumb, this date is the fourth day of the new fiscal month at least two full months from now. The cut-over should take about 3 and a half days and should be performed after the close of one fiscal month and before the commencement of operations in the next fiscal month.

For example, if today is February 19th, I would choose the First week of May for the Go-Live. I would use the rest of February for planning and sending out the preparation package to the managers of the new site. I would also use this time to visit the new site and present the kick-off meeting presentation. The project would begin the first week of March and the new users would be transacting in our SAP system in the first week of May.

For companies running on a 4-4-5 fiscal calendar, this is easy. The last day of the fiscal period is always a Friday. The cut-over would happen over the weekend and by Tuesday, the new users would be transacting on the system with only one business day (Monday) of down-time.

Of course, this is where we have to consider other things on the calendar such as holidays, the fiscal quarter and the cyclical trends in your industry.

Do not put it off too long. No time is a good time for a huge project, so pick the best time within the next few months. The sooner it is done, the better for all who are involved and the better for the company as a whole. This is another benefit of a 2 month implementation. This is going to be painful. The longer a project is drawn out, the longer the pain lasts. This pain affects a lot of people. The SAP team members, key users and champions as well as everyone involved at the new site and everyone throughout the company working with the processes which involve dealing with entities at an arm's reach. The faster the systems are integrated the faster you can enjoy the benefits of transacting and reporting from a single system.

Once the go-live date is selected, work backwards to the starting point. One can literally do this by drawing lines with arrows on a calendar and writing in the high level stages of the plan. Also draw in the milestones such as when the configuration will be a transported to QA and to Production as well as the go-live date. When I perform project planning like this, I will transfer this to a digital format to present in a presentation. Figure 3.3 shows an example of the digital format of the plan that started out as scratches on a real calendar. The rectangles with wording depict at a high-level the activity that will happen during each week. The ovals with percentages depict the level of involvement (as a percentage of time) we will need from key users during each activity.

Process Discovery & Integration – week 1

During the 1st week of the project, we learn as much as we can about the entity that will be moving to SAP. If they have documented their processes, we review those "AS-IS" processes to determine where we may have significant differences. If they are a manufacturer, we consider the manufacturing lead time of their products, their current fiscal calendar, and much more. During this week, we review the answers to the questionnaires that were sent to them with the project preparation package. If the SAP BSAs have questions, they contact the people within that organization to get as many questions answered as possible. Ideally the BSAs would be at the new location, but in reality most of this is done over the phone and via email.

Week 1 is also time to start looking at the data to determine which data objects need to be loaded in the SAP system and how each object will get loaded. This will be discussed in Chapter 5 "The Detailed Project Plan", but it is worth mentioning here because the results of this detailed effort are utilized in future weeks and highlighted in the high level plan.

Figure 3.3a High Level Project Plan (Calendar Version, Month 1)

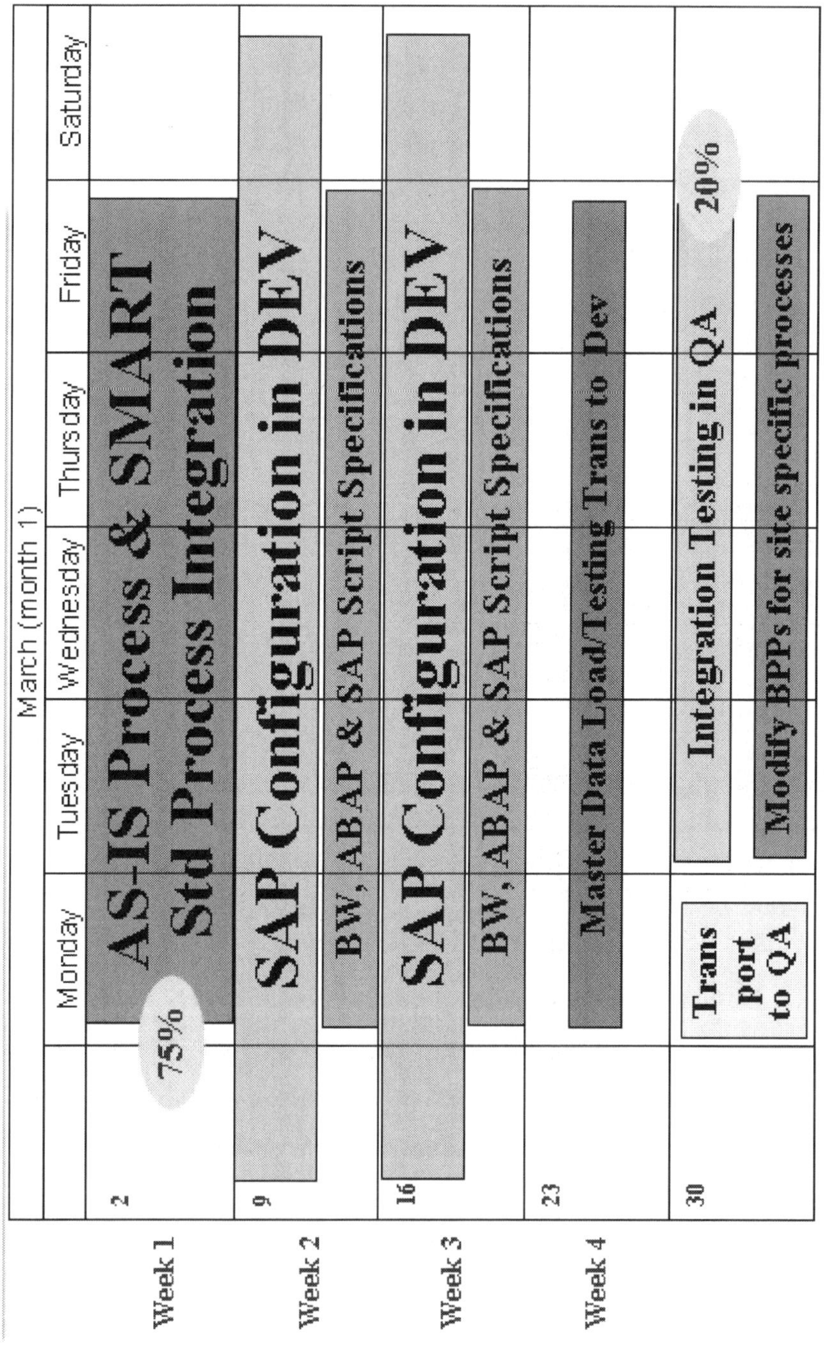

March (month 1)
Monday
Tuesday
Wednesday
Thursday
Friday
Saturday
Week 1
2
AS-IS Process & SMART
Std Process Integration
75%
Week 2
9
SAP Configuration in DEV
BW, ABAP & SAP Script Specifications
Week 3
16
SAP Configuration in DEV
BW, ABAP & SAP Script Specifications
Week 4
23
Master Data Load/Testing Trans to Dev
30
Trans port to QA
Integration Testing in QA
20%
Modify BPPs for site specific processes

Figure 3.3b High Level Project Plan (Calendar Version, Month 2)

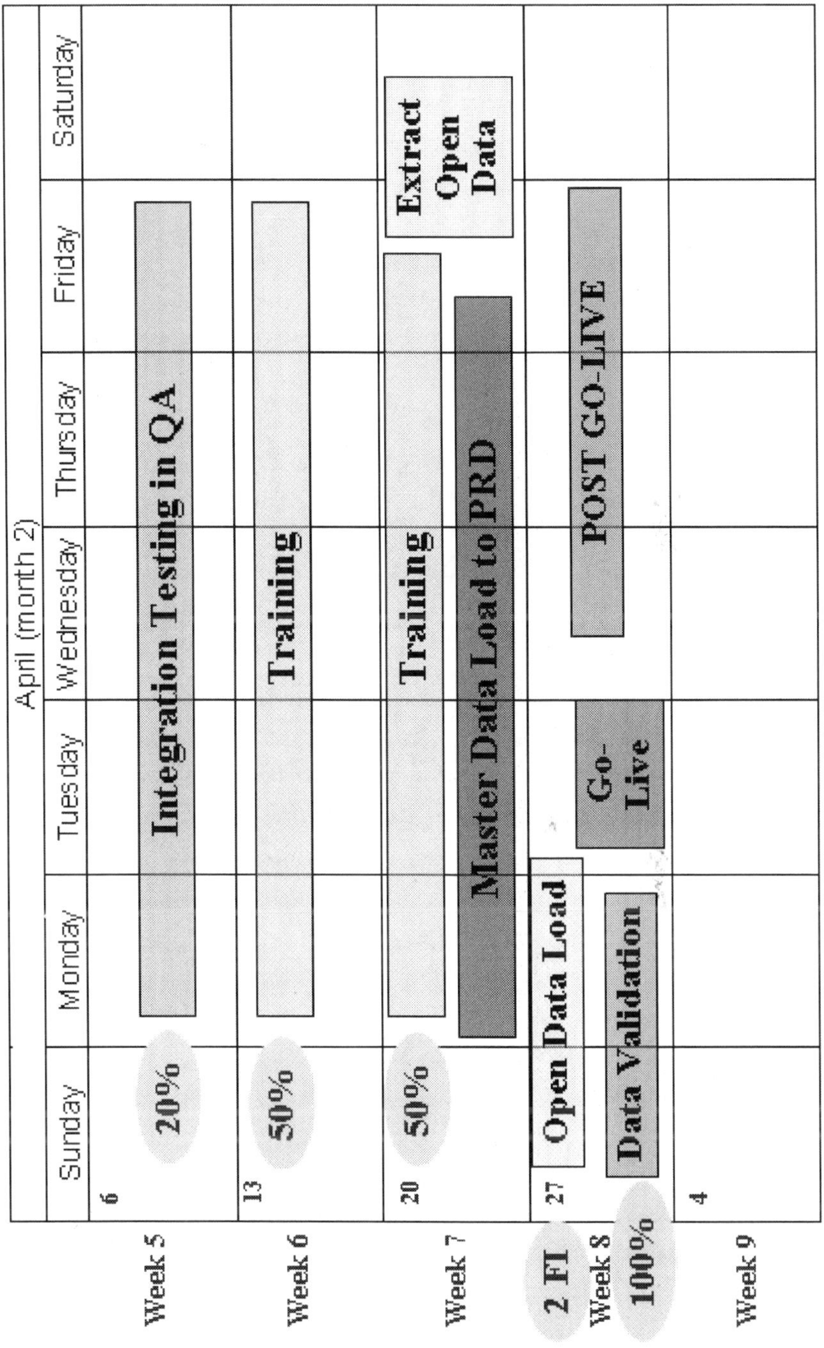

Configuration & Unit Testing – weeks 2 & 3

During the 2nd and 3rd weeks of the project, the BSAs perform the applicable configuration for things such as the new company code, sales organization, plant ID, account assignments, etc. The configuration performed at this stage is for the most part a copy of the configuration from the sister site. If any known process variations exist where a decision has been made to accommodate the differences, that configuration can be performed at this time as well. Of course, we avoid these differences if at all possible.

Sometimes we have to accommodate irregularities in our standard configuration for new entities. For example, when we implemented SAP in Brazil, there were localization OSS notes that needed to be applied. Local laws may require differences between sites that are unavoidable. I had a lot of experience implementing SAP in only 2 months, but for Brazil, I allotted 3 months.

We usually rollout SAP using an internal team, but for Brazil, I supplemented my team with a local consulting company because my team was not familiar with the Brazilian configuration and local legal requirements. It was very difficult to find a company in Brazil that would help us implement SAP in only 3 months. Most of them laughed at the idea of such a fast implementation. However, BBKO, a consulting firm in Brazil, was willing to give it a try. To this day, I know of no other company that has pulled off a 3 month implementation with Brazilian localization. We followed as many of our standard corporate processes and configuration as we could, but accommodated Brazilian localization where required. I am very proud of our 3 month implementation in Brazil, but obviously I cannot count it as one of my ten 2 month implementations.

Once the functionality is configured in the development system, the BSAs will perform unit testing to ensure the configuration works properly.

Also in weeks 2 & 3, the technical team will be busy as

well. They need to consider any changes that may be required to reports to include the new entity. At this time we also consider output differences. Sometimes when acquiring a new company, we decide to keep the brand name of the acquired company, so we need to print their logo on documents which will be seen by customers and suppliers such as sales order acknowledgements, packing lists, purchase orders, and invoices. This will require minor modifications to our standard documents. Sometimes we need to make accommodations to print different languages.

Technically the team can perform the changes and unit tests remotely. They do not have to be on-site at the new facility during this stage. But when this is done, it's time to get people on-site to help prepare the new company for what's coming.

Master Data Load – week 4

In week 4 we begin to perform test data loads in our development system. Master data includes objects such as customer master records, vendor master records, material master records, bills of materials, etc. This information is utilized when creating transactions in SAP. For example, to create a sales order, you need to have customer information and part numbers in the system. This master data needs to be mapped into SAP. We utilize data migration templates and data load programs. During week 4, we will begin to see if the maps that we generated were correct and if the load programs are working properly. Entering or loading the new company's information in our development system also helps to ensure that the configuration is correct.

Milestone – Transport to QA – beginning of week 5

As soon as we have tested the functionality in the development environment and know that the configuration is working, it is transported to the QA environment. This will allow us to begin to test and train the new users in the QA systems. It is important to keep track of all of the transports that are related to the project and move them to QA at the same time. If any transports are missing, we will learn this during the move to QA. This is the opportunity to learn from this mistake and make sure they are grouped and sequenced appropriately prior to the move to Production.

There are a couple of good practices for transport management that will make your life easier. First, all BSAs performing configuration for the project, should include the project name at the beginning of each transport description. Second, the basis person, working with the BSAs should maintain a transport list of all transports that are related to the project and they should be maintained in the appropriate order. With this list, the basis person can create a single transport which includes all transports for the project (or all transports that need to be moved together in the appropriate sequence).

The high level project plan should include a milestone where all transports are moved to QA. Once all of the transports are in QA, the integration testing begins.

Integration Testing - week 5

After transporting the configuration changes to the QA environment, the BSAs perform a quick test to ensure that everything transported properly and the system is working as expected. Then the integration testing can commence. I use the terms "integration testing" and "user acceptance testing" (UAT) synonymously. Although technically these can be two separate test streams, in a 2 month implementation, we perform integration testing and user acceptance testing in at the same time in a single track. In this streamlined approach we have the users test and prove that the SAP application modules and components and any other integrated application used for the business processes work together seamlessly from the end to end.

Integration testing is performed on-site at the new location. The champions lead the key users through the integration testing. These tests are performed by the business users, not by the SAP team. The SAP team will have worked with the champions and the key users to modify previously existing integration test scripts to accommodate the data in the new site. As the tests are being performed in the war room, we are getting the users to sign-off on each successful step of the test scripts. In the end, we will have SOX compliant proof of user acceptance testing.

During this stage, the key users lean heavily on the champions. This is often the first time some of these people have seen SAP. The champions use the integration testing as an opportunity to start training the key users.

This is usually when the s*@!t hits the fan! The magnitude of what is coming starts to hit the key users. They start to see how their processes will change. They start to think of details they had overlooked earlier. They begin to ask an enormous amount of questions. At this stage, concerns will escalate to senior management at the new site. This is when it starts to get exciting. It is the job of every experienced person on the project to resolve issues and concerns as they come up. By doing so, you will reassure them that everything will work out fine.

It is almost a given that there will be business issues that crop up during integration testing. It will take some time to resolve them and modify any configuration that did not work properly. These issues will be resolved and the system changes will need to be re-tested. Usually this means that integration testing extends into week 6 and overlaps with the first week of training.

Training – weeks 6 & 7

Training, as you would expect, is also a critical element of a successful implementation. Depending on the number of people that need to be trained in each department, it can be performed at different locations. Some training can be performed one-on-one or two-on-one at people's desks. Some training can be performed in the war room. Ideally, the site has a training room or a conference room that, with the addition of some PCs, can be used for training. Usually it is the champion that is performing the training, but the appropriate BSA also attends the training to answer any questions that arise which the champion is unprepared to deal with.

Transport to Production – Milestone - end of week 6

The configuration must be transported to production prior to beginning the master data loads. Therefore, the transports occur well before the cut-over weekend. The transport list must show which transports will go to production early to accommodate the master data load.

When the transports are moved to production, other people throughout the entire organization will be able to see the entries for the new company in the drop-down lists and on reports (even though there is no data yet). Security will have to be tight to ensure that no one from other sites makes entries in the new location before you are ready.

Master Data Load – week 7

This is the real deal. It is time to start loading master data in preparation for go-live. Objects that that need to be loaded using data load programs are tested again quickly in QA and then loaded into the Production SAP environment. (Remember, the real testing of the data load would have already happened during the integration testing. But I recommend one last sample load in QA prior to the loading the master data in Production.) As each object gets loaded, the users need to validate the data that was loaded. This is the beginning of the cut-over. Details will be covered in Chapter 5 "The Detailed Project Plan" and Chapter 11 "The Cut-over Plan".

Extract Open Data – end of week 7

Open data refers to transactional data or data generated by transactions in the system. Purchase orders, sales orders, and G/L account balances are examples of open data. In order to capture all of the open data, it must be done after the close of business during the cut-over. Once the last transaction in the legacy system is performed, we can begin to extract the open data and prepare it for loading into SAP. The open financial data can only be extracted after the financial close is complete.

Open Data Load & Data Validation – beginning of week 8

The real testing of the open data loads happened during the integration testing. But during the cut-over, a sample of the open data is again quickly test-loaded in the QA system. When the sample load in QA is successful, the entire open data files are loaded into the production system. As soon as each object is loaded, it is validated by business users. Once the business users sign-off on the data load, a final Go-No-Go decision is made. When the decision is a "Go", the final transport is moved to production and the new plant is officially live on SAP!

On your mark, get set, Go-Live!

Chapter 4
The Kick-off Presentation

"To dare is to lose one's footing momentarily. To not dare is to lose oneself."

– Soren Keirkegaard

The kick-off presentation on a 2 month SAP implementation is one of the most difficult presentations I have ever had to give. To start with, the room is full of skeptics. Often, I am in a room full of people who were just acquired by another company. This is already a negative in many people's mind. Now I am the bad guy from "Corporate" that is coming down to force them on to a new system that they don't think they need. Not only are they skeptical about moving onto a new system, but to do it in an impossible 8 weeks – NO WAY!

Actually the scenario above is a walk in the park compared to a couple of scenario's I have been through. On one occasion, my company had been acquired by another much larger company. However, we decided to rollout our SAP system to all of the entities in our newly created business unit which included manufacturing plants and distribution centers that were part of the core operations of the larger company before the acquisition. When I went to implement SAP at a fairly significant corporate site that had recently been added to our business unit, the response I got was something like, "Wait a minute, *we* own *you*! *We* bought *you* and now *you* are telling *us* what system to use and *you* are telling *us* what business processes to follow. I don't think so!" You can imagine how fun that meeting was.

In a similar scenario, one of the companies was based in Munich, Germany. They were also added to our business unit and they had already been using SAP for 9 years (since the R/2 days). While I was there my boss laid off the SAP Manager, and asked me to take over his job. My objective was to roll out our much less mature SAP environment to their facilities in Munich, California, and Japan. They had been part of the larger organization for several years before we were acquired. I could try to describe to you, but still you can only imagine the challenges that I faced dealing with that scenario.

With those kinds of experiences, I can attest that a presentation to a company you have recently acquired or even to another plant that has been part of the company, but not yet on SAP is much easier. Still it requires much tack, a lot of preparation, and the ability to read the audience to judge the appropriate amount of humor to include in the delivery of the kick-off presentation. It is a serious business, but if used properly, humor can be just the thing you need to make it out of the meeting relatively unscathed. (That and a fast getaway car would be helpful too.) ☺

The Audience

It is important to have the right people in the kick-off meeting. All of the managers of the new site should attend as well as all of the key users who will be directly involved in the project. If you are presenting, but you are not going to manage the project, it would be good to have your project manager in the meeting as well. In fact, the project manager should be a co-presenter. It is also important to have another senior manager from corporate present as well. A senior manager should convey that the project has the support of corporate management. It would be good to have the whole team including the champions and the SAP team in the meeting, but it is not required. Generally the kick-off meeting occurs well before the team lands on-site. Whether or not the champions and SAP team attends depends on the proximity of the sister site in relation to the new site and your travel budget.

The Message

The way you deliver the message is almost as important as the message itself. This section outlines the key content of the kick-off presentation as well as tips on the delivery of the content. The kick-off presentation is designed to let the team know what is involved in the project. It should include slides covering the following topics.

Global SAP Footprint: There should be a slide depicting your global SAP footprint. It should show all of your sites connected together and connected to a single instance of SAP. This shows that all sites can be connected to a single global instance and operate without fear of network latency problems. It also shows that all of these entities can run their business processes on a single global instance of SAP.

Implementation History: You should have a slide showing your achievements thus far implementing SAP, upgrading SAP, and any other relevant, major accomplishments. While showing this slide, you will want to instill upon the audience the amount of experience you and the team has had implementing SAP. You need to show your confidence in being able to meet your goal of implementing SAP at their site with a 2 month project plan.

The IT Organization Chart: It would be good to have a slide showing the IT organization chart including the executive that IT reports to. This shows them the person at the top who is the right person to talk to if something goes wrong. ☺ It also gives them an idea of the staff members that support SAP at your company.

Multiple ERP Landscape: I like to have a slide showing how other companies have different ERP systems around the world and the cons of having multiple ERPs within an organization.
The cons include things like:
- *Sites do not have visibility to activities at other sites.*
- *Data inconsistency between sites or regions*
- *Business Process inconsistency between sites or regions*
- *Multiple IT Teams are required to maintain systems.*
- *Additional staff is required to perform arms-reach transactions between the company's plants and distribution centers.*

Single Instance Landscape: I include a slide depicting the pros of a single instance landscape. I talk about the SAP NetWeaver® platform and how the applications on NetWeaver are built to work together. A single instance of each of the SAP products gives companies a single version of the truth. I list pros such as:
- *Single hardware system across all sites*
- *Single source of record for all master data*
    Customers, Vendors, Materials, BOMs, etc.
- *Single source of record for all transactions*
- *Synchronized business processes across all sites*
- *Automated inter-company transactions between sites*

Project Introduction: I include a slide with the project name and if there is a good story behind it, I let people know how and why the project was named. I also make it clear that the intent is to implement SAP at their site. Here you can discuss the scope (which SAP applications will be included and which applications will wait until a later date). Sometimes we implement our shop floor control system at the same time, but not always. It is important that the scope is clearly defined and communicated up front.

The SMART Approach: I generally show a slide that outlines the SMART Approach to implementing SAP. It includes the following:

- *Blueprint – Design Document (~ 1 week)*
  - *Review "AS-IS" processes. Share corporate standard processes.*
- *Configuration (~ 1-2 weeks)*
  - *Copy configuration from sister plant*
- *Test (~ 3-4 weeks)*
  - *Unit test in DEV*
  - *Integration test / UAT in QA*
- *Training (~ 2 weeks)*
  - *Performed in the final 2 weeks of the project*
- *Data Migration (~ 4 weeks)*
- *Cut-Over (long weekend)*

The Project Plan: I show the high level project plan which outlines the 2 month implementation and the high level activities that will be happening in each week. It often shows what level of business resources will be needed each week. I generally show a slide for each month in a calendar format. There is an example of this in Chapter 3 "Project Preparation". Sometimes I also show it in a Gantt chart format.

Contingency Plan: It is comforting for them to see the contingency plan so I usually include a slide showing when we would go-live if we missed our initial target. I explain that we must go live over a fiscal period end. Even though you don't plan to use the contingency plan, you still need to put some thought into it. (Knock on wood, but I have yet to use a contingency plan, but it gives them comfort in knowing that we have one.)

The Implementation Team: There should be a slide showing who the players will be; the SAP team members and IT consultants (if any) as well as the project sponsors. I also show a slide of the key users from the new site and the business area they are expected to cover. At this time I ask for confirmation that the key user-to-business area mapping is correct.

The Buddy System: It is important to show a slide that partners people together from the sister site. It shows which plant is their sister site and the names, phone numbers and email addresses of their buddies at the sister site.

Next Steps: This slide will show the activities that will happen following the kick-off meeting.

Jump Start: I include a list of the activities that they can get started on prior to the team landing on site to start the project. It includes the jump start activities from the preparation package.
- ✓ *Confirm Chart of Accounts mapping to Corporate Chart of Accounts*
- ✓ *Complete the System Integration Questionnaire*
- ✓ *Complete the contact information template (key user listing)*
- ✓ *Compare Material Masters for component matching (Same components will be extended from Corporate or the plant of record. Different components are created as required.)*

Q&A: The final slide is for the Questions & Answers session.

Obviously you should customize the presentation to the specific circumstances you are dealing with. But the message is critical. In this meeting the broader audience starts to get an idea of the magnitude of the project. They realize they will be going through a major change. If you deliver the message well, they will also realize that other sites or at least other companies have been through this before and are better off because of it. This is the opportunity to get their buy in on the approach.

This is also a great opportunity to begin to build support and momentum for the project. If you deliver the presentation well, they get excited about the project. They get excited about the challenge. They are concerned, but excited.

It is important to tell them that this project will not be an easy project. It will not be perfect. It will be painful, but I promise that we will not leave them hanging out to dry. We will not implement a new system and give them no support. It will be one of the most difficult things a company will endure. But they will come out of it stronger. They will come out of it with a sense of accomplishment and it gives all of the new employees something in common. It will be very tough, but they will look back on it as exciting and for many even fun.

Not only will the site be stronger, and the people within the site will be a stronger team, but the entire company will be stronger. The entire company will have something in common. What they will have in common is not only a single global instance of SAP, but also a community of people sharing their experiences with their coworkers around the globe. This community begins to share more than their SAP implementation experiences. They also start to share their business process experiences. This in turn, makes the company even stronger and more agile. The people within the organization have more than an industry language in common and more than an SAP language in common. They have a company language mixing both industry and SAP terms. They can migrate product lines from one plant to another easily. They can share human resources easily. The entire organization gains a synergy that gives the company a competitive advantage in the marketplace.

This is a great advantage for the company, but the experience can also be a great asset for the people involved in the implementation. These people will have something in common with all of the people in the SAP community. They can join SAP user groups and gain experiences from people all over the world from many different industries in many different positions who all have something in common. They all have experience and even provide input in SAP products and services. Organizations such as ASUG (America's SAP User Group) provide input to SAP. ASUG has influence sessions where people come together and make recommendations which could be included in future releases of SAP products.

People begin to realize that being a part of an SAP implementation can open opportunities for them within the organization. They can become part of the company's continuous improvement program. They can become members of the champion community. They can even become members of a much larger community; the SAP community. They can share information with other companies and learn from other companies' experiences. It introduces them to a network of people they have something in common with. I have found that people in the SAP community are often willing to share their experiences not just with SAP software and business processes, but with other industry challenges they may have faced.

The kick-off presentation is an opportunity to introduce the audience to the world of SAP and your company's involvement in the SAP community.

Chapter 5
The Detailed Project Plan

"Do not go where the path may lead, go instead where there is no path and leave a trail."

– Ralph Waldo Emerson

The project plan is a living, breathing document. It lives throughout the entire project. The project plan used as an example in this book depicts the project as underway.

This chapter contains the detailed project plan with explanations of the tasks defined in the plan. Unlike the high level project plan, the detailed plan is not used for estimating the timeline of general project areas or for presentations. Instead the detailed project plan shows step-by-step everything required for a successful implementation following the SMART Approach. It shows in detail, not just the steps required, but also the duration of each step. It identifies who is to perform each step and what (if any) prerequisites are required before performing each step. The detailed project plan can also be used for resource planning to ensure that people (resources) are not stretched too thin.

Task #1 simply shows that our goal is to configure and implement SAP for Company Code 06.

Task # 2 - # 3, Planning Phase: In this first week of the project, begin the planning phase by copying the project plan from a previous 2 month implementation, to create a new plan for the new implementation. Then massage the plan to fit the new project. This is much faster than creating a project plan from scratch for each implementation.

Task # 4 - #8, Identify Integration Team: The "Integration Team", is the SAP team who will be working on this project. When choosing the team members, you need to take into consideration all of the other projects that are underway and the workload of the entire team. Sometimes it is important to consider languages. If multi-lingual resources are available and the implementation is in a region that speaks the same or similar language, it will help to include at least one person on the team who speaks that language. When we implemented SAP in Puerto Rico and Brazil, we had Spanish-speaking team members. Even though Brazilians speak Portuguese, Spanish was a close enough fit. They could communicate effectively and if they had questions, they understood enough to ask each other. It is also important to consider global regions. It obviously saves on travel costs if the resources are local. Finally, consider the personal family and health issues that each team member may be dealing with to make sure they are able to travel. The goal is to find one person to cover each SAP module. You will find more information about the team in Chapter 3 "Project Preparation".

Task # 10 - #12, Issue Resolution Process: It is always good to define upfront how issues will be tracked and escalated during the project. During this phase make sure to have a fresh issues log posted to a public place where the entire team can maintain entries and updated the status of issues. The location of the issues log is circulated so everyone knows where to find it. This is also the phase where calendar notifications of periodic team meetings are sent out. Microsoft SharePoint is a great tool for maintaining Issues Logs, Project Calendars, and Project Documents. In the beginning, the meetings are weekly and somewhat limited to the SAP team. Once we get on site, the meetings include the champions, key users, and some members of the local management team. When we get on site, the meetings migrate from weekly to daily.

Figure 5.1 Sample Project Plan (tasks 1 –22)

#	% Work Complete	⊙	Task Name	Duration	Start	Finish
1	75%		Project: Company 06	23 days?	Mon 2/4/08	Wed 3/5/08
2	75%		Planning Phase	23 days?	Mon 2/4/08	Wed 3/5/08
3	11%		Prepare Project Plan	4 days	Tue 2/26/08	Fri 2/29/08
4	100%		Identify Integration Team	20 days?	Mon 2/4/08	Fri 2/29/08
5	100%	✓	Identify BSA Team	4 days?	Tue 2/26/08	Fri 2/29/08
6	100%	✓	Identify ABAP Developers	4 days?	Tue 2/26/08	Fri 2/29/08
7	100%	▦	Identify Sister site and Champion Users	4 days?	Mon 2/4/08	Thu 2/7/08
8	100%	▦	Identify Key Users	4 days	Tue 2/26/08	Fri 2/29/08
9						
10	100%	✓	Issue Resolution Process	1 day?	Wed 3/5/08	Wed 3/5/08
11	100%	✓	Implement Issue Tracking System	1 day?	Wed 3/5/08	Wed 3/5/08
12	100%	✓	Set up time for periodic meetings	1 day	Wed 3/5/08	Wed 3/5/08
13						
14	100%		Preliminary Preparation	50 days?	Tue 2/26/08	Fri 5/2/08
15	100%		Develop Infrastructure Plan	50 days?	Tue 2/26/08	Fri 5/2/08
16	100%	✓	Connectivity Dates - March 26	14 days?	Tue 3/4/08	Fri 3/21/08
17	100%	✓	Desktop Upgrade/Replacement Plan	14 days?	Thu 3/6/08	Tue 3/25/08
18	100%	✓	Identify Printers for SAP Printing	1 day?	Tue 3/11/08	Tue 3/11/08
19	100%	✓	Invoices - Pre-printed Forms / Checks - Pre-printed A4 size forms	1 day?	Tue 3/11/08	Tue 3/11/08
20	100%	✓	Shipping / Receiving / Stock Room - Laser (need)	1 day?	Tue 3/11/08	Tue 3/11/08
21	100%	✓	Label Printer - Zebra (need)	1 day?	Tue 3/11/08	Tue 3/11/08
22	100%	✓	Purchase Orders - Pre-printed forms	1 day?	Tue 3/11/08	Tue 3/11/08

Task # 14 - # 22, Develop Infrastructure Plan: Very early in the project, consider the network connectivity to the new site, the PCs and the printers. There is a long lead time on the WAN connectivity, so the order needs to be placed with the telecommunications carrier early in the project. Sometimes we set up a temporary VPN for quicker access. The PCs need to be evaluated to ensure they are sized appropriately to handle the SAP desktop footprint. If necessary, plan to replace the older machines or upgrade the memory. It is time to get the hardware on order and schedule time to upgrade the machines. At this time determine the status of the printers. It is a good idea to standardize on the make and model of networkable printers. If you have a standard printer platform, the outputs will be more predictable. It is important to determine if more printers will be necessary to print appropriate documents in the appropriate areas throughout the building(s).

Figure 5.2 Sample Project Plan (tasks 25 –48)

	% Work Complete	ⓘ	Task Name	Duration	Start	Finish
25	**100%**	✓	**⊟ Record Major Decisions and Directions**	**4 days?**	**Tue 2/26/08**	**Fri 2/29/08**
26	100%	✓	Company Code: 06	4 days	Tue 2/26/08	Fri 2/29/08
27	100%	✓	Logos on SAPScripts (Artwork)	4 days?	Tue 2/26/08	Fri 2/29/08
28	100%	✓	Actual Costing - Current Standard costing for assemblies includes labor & ov	4 days?	Tue 2/26/08	Fri 2/29/08
29						
30	**100%**		**⊟ Data Migration**	**46 days?**	**Mon 3/3/08**	**Fri 5/2/08**
31	**100%**	✓	**⊟ Define Master Data Extract / Load / Delete Approaches by Object**	**10 days**	**Mon 3/3/08**	**Fri 3/14/08**
32	100%	✓	Material Master - Extract / Load	5.33 days	Mon 3/3/08	Mon 3/10/08
33	100%	✓	Material Classification - Id by Matl / Extract / Load	5 days	Mon 3/3/08	Fri 3/7/08
34	100%	✓	BOMs - Extract / Load	10 days	Mon 3/3/08	Fri 3/14/08
35	100%	✓	Work Centers - Manual Create in 06	5 days	Mon 3/3/08	Fri 3/7/08
36	100%	✓	Routings - Manual create in Company 06	5 days	Mon 3/3/08	Fri 3/7/08
37	100%	✓	Vendor Master - Manual	10 days	Mon 3/3/08	Fri 3/14/08
38	100%	✓	Purchasing Info Records - (Volume ~ 230) - Manual with SMART's he	5 days	Mon 3/3/08	Fri 3/7/08
39	100%	✓	Customer Master - Manual	5 days	Mon 3/3/08	Fri 3/7/08
40	100%	✓	Customer Credit Limit - Manual	5 days	Mon 3/3/08	Fri 3/7/08
41	100%	✓	Freight Carriers - Manual	5 days	Mon 3/3/08	Fri 3/7/08
42	100%	✓	Customer Material Infor Records - Manual	5 days	Mon 3/3/08	Fri 3/7/08
43	100%	✓	Pricing - Manual pricing	5 days	Mon 3/3/08	Fri 3/7/08
44	100%	✓	GL Accounts - SAP Std Program	5 days	Mon 3/3/08	Fri 3/7/08
45	100%	✓	Cost Centers - Manual	5 days	Mon 3/3/08	Fri 3/7/08
46	100%	✓	Cost Elements - Manual	5 days	Mon 3/3/08	Fri 3/7/08
47	100%	✓	Profit Centers - Manual	5 days	Mon 3/3/08	Fri 3/7/08
48	100%	✓	Fixed Assets - Extract / Load	5 days	Mon 3/3/08	Fri 3/7/08

Task # 25 - # 28, Record Major Decisions and Directions: In this section of the plan, it is a good idea to list major decisions that everyone on the team needs to know about. For example, the company code, sales organization, and plant ID which will be used to configure the new site. Another example is whether or not the new acquisition will continue to use their logo or if they will be doing business under the corporate logo. (This is important for the outputs that will be seen by the customers.) We also need to confirm that the company will be running on an actual costing model or a standard costing model and if the company will be running a Make-to-Order scenario or a Build-to-Stock scenario. As long as there is a standard configuration sets in your system to accommodate each of these options. The choice of the sister site is included in this section. (The configuration is copied from the sister site which is also the site where the champions are from.)

Task # 30 - # 48, Master Data Extraction / Load Approach: Here we list all of the master data objects that must be considered during the project. For each object, we need to decide if we need to migrate it to SAP or not. If it needs to be migrated to the SAP, we need to decide:

1. Will it be extracted by a program or manually?
2. Will it be loaded to SAP via a program or manually entered?

To determine this, I use a rule of thumb. If there are less than 300 records, it will be loaded manually. The thought is that if there are less than 300 records to load, they can be manually entered by a business user faster than it will take the SAP team to write or modify and test a program to load the data. If there are more than 300 records, we will determine if it can be loaded via LSMW (SAP's Legacy System Migration Warehouse). If not, we will need to create a load program or modify one we have used in the past. Depending on the object, the load program could be a BDC program which loads records screen by screen or preferably a direct update program which loads records directly to the tables and structures in SAP.

Figure 5.3 Sample Project Plan (tasks 50 –63)

	% Work Complete	❶	Task Name	Duration	Start	Finish
50	100%	✓	⊟ **Define Open Data Extract / Load / Delete Approaches by Object**	**5 days**	**Mon 3/3/08**	**Fri 3/7/08**
51	100%	✓	Purchase Orders - Id by Material / Extract / Manual Load	5 days	Mon 3/3/08	Fri 3/7/08
52	100%	✓	MRO Purchase Orders - ID by Cost Center / Manual Load	5 days	Mon 3/3/08	Fri 3/7/08
53	100%	✓	Production Orders - ID by Matl / Manual	5 days	Mon 3/3/08	Fri 3/7/08
54	100%	✓	Inventory - 561 in 06 and 562 in 06 / Load	5 days	Mon 3/3/08	Fri 3/7/08
55	100%	✓	Sales Orders - Determine Volume / Manual	5 days	Mon 3/3/08	Fri 3/7/08
56	100%	✓	GL Account Balances - Extract / Load	5 days	Mon 3/3/08	Fri 3/7/08
57	100%	✓	AR Sub-Ledger - Extract / Load	5 days	Mon 3/3/08	Fri 3/7/08
58	100%	✓	AP Sub-Ledger - Extract / Load	5 days	Mon 3/3/08	Fri 3/7/08
59	100%	✓	Fixed Assets - Extract / Load	5 days	Mon 3/3/08	Fri 3/7/08
60						
61	100%	✓	Send Specifications to Programmers	1 day?	Wed 3/12/08	Wed 3/12/08
62	100%	✓	Write Extract Programs	8 days	Wed 3/12/08	Fri 3/21/08
63	100%	✓	Test Extract Programs	3 days	Mon 3/24/08	Wed 3/26/08

Task # 50 - # 59, Define Open Data Extract / Load Approach: Open data is created by transactions in SAP. Therefore, open data will need to be migrated during the cut-over weekend to ensure we do not lose any data from the transactions in the legacy system. There will be much less time to load transaction data. Therefore, it is a given that we will extract and load financial data during the cut-over and this will be done via programs. Still, these programs need to be tested to ensure that we capture all of the data and to ensure that the balances are correct after they have been loaded.   Open Purchase Orders and Sales Orders can be loaded manually depending on the volume of orders. Orders that we know will not be transacted on before the cutover <u>and</u> will still be open after the cutover can be moved over somewhat early as long as the supporting master data exists in the SAP. This would be the case for orders that will not ship until after go-live based on the lead time of the materials or the customer's requested ship date.

Task # 61 - # 63, Programs: This section reminds us that we will need time write or update extract programs and load programs for the objects that were determined to require programs.

Figure 5.4 Sample Project Plan (tasks 65 –91)

	% Work Complete	ⓘ	Task Name	Duration	Start	Finish
65	100%	✓	⊟ Configuration	15 days ?	Mon 3/3/08	Fri 3/21/08
66	100%	✓	⊟ MM	10 days	Mon 3/3/08	Fri 3/14/08
67	100%	✓	Plant Code	10 days	Mon 3/3/08	Fri 3/14/08
68	100%	✓	Storage Locations	10 days	Mon 3/3/08	Fri 3/14/08
69	100%	✓	Buyer Codes / MRP Controller Codes	10 days	Mon 3/3/08	Fri 3/14/08
70	100%	✓	Review SAPScripts	10 days	Mon 3/3/08	Fri 3/14/08
71	100%	✓	⊟ PP	10 days	Mon 3/3/08	Fri 3/14/08
72	100%	✓	Shop Floor Tracking System	10 days	Mon 3/3/08	Fri 3/14/08
73	100%	✓	⊟ SD	10 days	Mon 3/3/08	Fri 3/14/08
74	100%	✓	Sales Organization	10 days	Mon 3/3/08	Fri 3/14/08
75	100%	✓	Sales Office Assignment	10 days	Mon 3/3/08	Fri 3/14/08
76	100%	✓	Distribution Channel Assignment	10 days	Mon 3/3/08	Fri 3/14/08
77	100%	✓	Division Assignment	10 days	Mon 3/3/08	Fri 3/14/08
78	100%	✓	Shipping Points Re-Assign	10 days	Mon 3/3/08	Fri 3/14/08
79	100%	✓	Loading Groups Re-Assign	10 days	Mon 3/3/08	Fri 3/14/08
80	100%	✓	Review SAPScripts	10 days	Mon 3/3/08	Fri 3/14/08
81	100%	✓	⊟ A/P	10 days	Mon 3/3/08	Fri 3/14/08
82	100%	✓	User Tolerances	10 days	Mon 3/3/08	Fri 3/14/08
83	100%	✓	⊟ A/R	10 days	Mon 3/3/08	Fri 3/14/08
84	100%	✓	AR User Tolerances	10 days	Mon 3/3/08	Fri 3/14/08
85	100%	✓	⊟ Profit Centers	10 days	Mon 3/3/08	Fri 3/14/08
86	100%	✓	Profit Center Structure	10 days	Mon 3/3/08	Fri 3/14/08
87	100%	✓	⊟ G/L & CO	10 days	Mon 3/3/08	Fri 3/14/08
88	100%	✓	Configure G/L Assignment	10 days	Mon 3/3/08	Fri 3/14/08
89	100%	✓	Account Determination SD (VKOA)	10 days	Mon 3/3/08	Fri 3/14/08
90	100%	✓	Account Determination MM (T030)	10 days	Mon 3/3/08	Fri 3/14/08
91	100%	✓	OKRS - Assign G/L Account	10 days	Mon 3/3/08	Fri 3/14/08

Task # 65 - # 91, Configuration: The plan calls for two weeks of SAP configuration. This includes creating the new Company Code, Plant, and Sales Organization in SAP. It includes extending the GL Accounts and the account assignments, etc. The items listed in this section are not necessarily a complete list, but are a good representation. By using a cookie-cutter approach, we should not have to create new Purchase Order types, Sales Order types, Work Order Types, item categories, etc. The plan is for the new company to use the same basic configuration as the rest of the sites. This saves a lot of time when configuring the system. It also promotes standard business processes throughout all sites which will save a lot of time when determining the "To-Be" processes.

Figure 5.5 Sample Project Plan (tasks 93 –111)

	% Work Complete	ⓘ	Task Name	Duration	Start	Finish
93	100%	✓	⊟ **Extend Master Data in DEV**	**5 days**	**Mon 3/24/08**	**Fri 3/28/08**
94	100%	✓	Material Master - Extend	5 days	Mon 3/24/08	Fri 3/28/08
95	100%	✓	BOMs - Allocate	5 days	Mon 3/24/08	Fri 3/28/08
96	100%	✓	Work Centers - Manual	5 days	Mon 3/24/08	Fri 3/28/08
97	100%	✓	Routings - Manual	5 days	Mon 3/24/08	Fri 3/28/08
98	100%	✓	Vendor Master - Extend	5 days	Mon 3/24/08	Fri 3/28/08
99	100%	✓	Purchasing Info Records - Load	5 days	Mon 3/24/08	Fri 3/28/08
100	100%	✓	Customer Master - Manual	5 days	Mon 3/24/08	Fri 3/28/08
101	100%	✓	Customer Credit Limit - Manual	5 days	Mon 3/24/08	Fri 3/28/08
102	100%	✓	Customer Material Info Records - Manual	5 days	Mon 3/24/08	Fri 3/28/08
103	100%	✓	Freight Carriers - Manual	5 days	Mon 3/24/08	Fri 3/28/08
104	100%	✓	Pricing - Manual	5 days	Mon 3/24/08	Fri 3/28/08
105	100%	✓	GL Accounts - Manual	5 days	Mon 3/24/08	Fri 3/28/08
106	100%	✓	Cost Centers - Manual	5 days	Mon 3/24/08	Fri 3/28/08
107	100%	✓	Cost Elements - Manual	5 days	Mon 3/24/08	Fri 3/28/08
108	100%	✓	Profit Centers - Manual	5 days	Mon 3/24/08	Fri 3/28/08
109						
110	100%	✓	Extract Open Data from PRD for testing	5 days	Mon 3/24/08	Fri 3/28/08
111	100%	✓	Prepare Data Files for Load	5 days	Mon 3/24/08	Fri 3/28/08

Task # 93 - # 108, Extend Master Data in DEV: After the configuration is done, it is time to load or extend master data in the development system. This is when we will find out if the master data configuration is correct. It is also when we confirm that the values in the master data templates and load files are correct.

Task # 110 - # 111, Open data preparation: Here we extract samples of open data for preparation to load. It takes time to ensure that the extract programs are correct, and to format the data for loading into SAP.

Task # 113 - # 120, Load Open Data in DEV: When we load open data into the SAP development system, we will be able to see if the configuration for open data is correct in SAP and we will confirm that the load programs work.

Task # 122, Perform Unit Testing: Unit testing is testing performed by the SAP team. This testing is not intended to prove the flow of transactions from the beginning to the end of a process like Integration testing does, but it ensures that each individual piece of the configuration is working as expected. Usually unit testing happens during the configuration stage, but we throw in another round of unit testing using the data that has been loaded with the load programs. I have seen a case where the testing went fine with data that was entered manually, but it failed when testing with data that was loaded via a load program. We need to know as early as possible if we have a situation like that.

Figure 5.6 Sample Project Plan (tasks 113 –131)

	% Work Complete	O	Task Name	Duration	Start	Finish
113	100%	✓	**Load Open Data in DEV**	**2 days?**	**Sat 3/29/08**	**Mon 3/31/08**
114	100%	✓	Purchase Orders	2 days?	Sat 3/29/08	Mon 3/31/08
115	100%	✓	Production Orders	2 days?	Sat 3/29/08	Mon 3/31/08
116	100%	✓	Inventory	2 days?	Sat 3/29/08	Mon 3/31/08
117	100%	✓	Sales Orders	2 days?	Sat 3/29/08	Mon 3/31/08
118	100%	✓	GL Account Balances	2 days?	Sat 3/29/08	Mon 3/31/08
119	100%	✓	AR Sub-Ledger	2 days?	Sat 3/29/08	Mon 3/31/08
120	100%	✓	AP Sub-Ledger	2 days?	Sat 3/29/08	Mon 3/31/08
121						
122	100%	✓	Perform Unit Testing in DEV (Loaded Data)	1 day	Fri 3/28/08	Fri 3/28/08
123						
124	100%	✓	Transport to QA	1 day	Mon 3/31/08	Mon 3/31/08
125						
126	100%	✓	**User Maintenance**	**12 days ?**	**Wed 3/19/08**	**Wed 4/2/08**
127	100%	✓	Get List of users to Basis & Security	1 day?	Wed 3/19/08	Wed 3/19/08
128	100%	✓	Edit Access in QA	5 days	Fri 3/28/08	Wed 4/2/08
129						
130	100%	✓	**Perform Unit Testing in QA**	**3 days**	**Tue 4/1/08**	**Thu 4/3/08**
131	100%	✓	Fix Config Problems	3 days	Tue 4/1/08	Thu 4/3/08

Task #124, Transport to QA: Once we are comfortable with the configuration in the SAP development system and we know that it works with both manually created data and data loaded via programs, it is time to move the configuration to the SAP QA systems for further testing and training of the new users. The configuration must be moved to QA before the data can be loaded into the QA system.

Task # 126 - # 128, User Maintenance: The Business Systems Analysts (BSAs) determine the SAP authorization roles that should be assigned to each person based on their job function. Matching the users to their counterparts in other plants makes this easier. The BSAs send this information to the Basis & Security person on a spreadsheet. The users must be created in QA and assigned the appropriate roles so they will have access during integration testing and training. An important part of the integration testing is not only to prove that the transactions and data work correctly, but also to determine if the users have appropriate SAP access. You don't want to go-live and suddenly find out that people do not have the access they need to perform critical business transactions. You also don't want to give them too much access. Not only could that grow into a Sarbanes-Oxley SOD (Segregation of Duties) violation, but new users are more likely to make mistakes. So it's best to ensure they have access only to the transactions that they need. User access needs to be approved by the BDOs (Business Data Owners) prior to go-live.

Task # 130 - #131, Perform Unit Testing in QA: Once the configuration has been moved to QA, it is a good idea to have the BSAs test it first before the users start testing. This is to make sure that all of the configuration was transported properly. It would be a shame to have scheduled the users for integration testing only to find that configuration was missing which prevented them from being able to test things properly. It would be a waste of everyone's time. If the BSAs find any errors in QA, they quickly fix it in the Development system, update the transport log and move the fix to QA.

Figure 5.7 Sample Project Plan (tasks 133 –157)

	% Work Complete	ⓘ	Task Name	Duration	Start	Finish
133	**100%**	✓	⊟ **Extend Master Data in QA**	**5 days**	**Mon 3/24/08**	**Fri 3/28/08**
134	100%	✓	Material Master	5 days	Mon 3/24/08	Fri 3/28/08
135	100%	✓	BOMs	5 days	Mon 3/24/08	Fri 3/28/08
136	100%	✓	Work Centers	5 days	Mon 3/24/08	Fri 3/28/08
137	100%	✓	Routings	5 days	Mon 3/24/08	Fri 3/28/08
138	100%	✓	Vendor Master	5 days	Mon 3/24/08	Fri 3/28/08
139	100%	✓	Purchasing Info Records	5 days	Mon 3/24/08	Fri 3/28/08
140	100%	✓	Customer Master	5 days	Mon 3/24/08	Fri 3/28/08
141	100%	✓	Customer Credit Limit	5 days	Mon 3/24/08	Fri 3/28/08
142	100%	✓	Customer Material Infor Records	5 days	Mon 3/24/08	Fri 3/28/08
143	100%	✓	Freight Carriers	5 days	Mon 3/24/08	Fri 3/28/08
144	100%	✓	Pricing	5 days	Mon 3/24/08	Fri 3/28/08
145	100%	✓	GL Accounts	5 days	Mon 3/24/08	Fri 3/28/08
146	100%	✓	Cost Centers	5 days	Mon 3/24/08	Fri 3/28/08
147	100%	✓	Cost Elements	5 days	Mon 3/24/08	Fri 3/28/08
148	100%	✓	Profit Centers	5 days	Mon 3/24/08	Fri 3/28/08
149						
150	**100%**	✓	⊟ **Load Open Data in QA**	**5 days**	**Mon 3/24/08**	**Fri 3/28/08**
151	100%	✓	Purchase Orders	5 days	Mon 3/24/08	Fri 3/28/08
152	100%	✓	Production Orders	5 days	Mon 3/24/08	Fri 3/28/08
153	100%	✓	Inventory	5 days	Mon 3/24/08	Fri 3/28/08
154	100%	✓	Sales Orders	5 days	Mon 3/24/08	Fri 3/28/08
155	100%	✓	GL Account Balances	5 days	Mon 3/24/08	Fri 3/28/08
156	100%	✓	AR Sub-Ledger	5 days	Mon 3/24/08	Fri 3/28/08
157	100%	✓	AP Sub-Ledger	5 days	Mon 3/24/08	Fri 3/28/08

Task # 133 - # 148, Extend Master Data in QA: Once the proper configuration is in QA, it is time to load the master data. Again this re-affirms that the configuration is correct and the load programs are working. It also shows that the data is formatted correctly for load. Some data can simply be extended from other plants. If the new manufacturing plant uses common components to manufacture their products, we would extend those material masters rather than loading new part numbers. (For details, see Chapter 10 "Data Migration".)

Task #150 - # 157, Load Open Data in QA: Once the master data is correct in QA, we can test our open data loads. This is critical because, as I mentioned before, we will be under a time crunch to get the open data loaded during the cutover weekend. We cannot afford avoidable surprises during cutover. There will be plenty of other surprises to deal with! ☺

Figure 5.8 Sample Project Plan (tasks 159 –173)

	% Work Complete	ⓘ	Task Name	Duration	Start	Finish
159	**100%**	✓	**Integration Testing**	**11 days**	**Mon 3/24/08**	**Fri 4/4/08**
160	100%	✓	Prepare Integration Test Scenarios	5 days	Mon 3/24/08	Fri 3/28/08
161	100%	✓	Perform Integration Tests in TRN100	5 days	Mon 3/31/08	Fri 4/4/08
162	100%	✓	Integration Test Sign-Off	1 day	Fri 4/4/08	Fri 4/4/08
163						
164						
165	100%	✓	Transport Configuration to PRD	1 day	Mon 4/21/08	Mon 4/21/08
166						
167						
168	**100%**	✓	**Final Preparation Phase**	**10 days**	**Mon 4/14/08**	**Fri 4/25/08**
169	100%	✓	Training - SAP	10 days	Mon 4/14/08	Fri 4/25/08
170	100%	✓	Training - Shop Floor Systems	10 days	Mon 4/14/08	Fri 4/25/08
171						
172	**100%**	✓	**User Maintenance**	**1 day**	**Thu 4/17/08**	**Thu 4/17/08**
173	100%	✓	Modify User Access in PRD	1 day	Thu 4/17/08	Thu 4/17/08

Task # 159 - # 162, Integration Testing: Integration testing / UAT (User Acceptance Testing) is testing performed by the users. Integration test scenarios are created for all business processes and they ensure that the processes are tested end-to-end. The test scripts need to be signed-off by the testers as the tests are completed successfully. These documents will be audited for SOX compliance.

Task # 165, Transport to PRD: Once we have completed the integration testing, it is time to move the configuration to the SAP production system. This needs to be done so we can begin to load or extend master data in Production. Master data is extended if the records already exist for another site. Otherwise it is loaded.

Task # 168 - # 170, Final Preparation Phase: Final preparation starts by training the users. There are two weeks allocated to end user training.

Task # 172 - # 173, User Maintenance: It is time to ensure that all new users are created in the SAP Production system and to ensure they have the appropriate authorization roles. Some key users may gain access early because they will be manually maintaining master data prior to go-live. It is important to stress to them that they should not perform any transactions at this time. The purpose for them to have access is only to load data. It is a good idea to create a special user ID for the load programs to utilize. I usually create an ID that represents the project name and load the data with that ID. After a couple of years have passed, if people question transactions, they will know that these transactions were loaded during the initial go-live. I learned this from experience. During my first project, the sales orders were loaded with my user ID. For a couple of years, people would come to me and question sales orders that I had entered. I had to explain that I did not know the details of the orders, but they were loaded from our legacy system during cut-over. In subsequent projects, I used a project user ID to avoid this confusion and it worked brilliantly.

Figure 5.9 Sample Project Plan (tasks 175 –200)

	% Work Complete	⊙	Task Name	Duration	Start	Finish
175	100%	✓	⊟ **Extend Master Data in PRD**	**4 days**	**Mon 4/21/08**	**Thu 4/24/08**
176	100%	✓	Material Master	4 days	Mon 4/21/08	Thu 4/24/08
177	100%	✓	BOMs	4 days	Mon 4/21/08	Thu 4/24/08
178	100%	✓	Work Centers	4 days	Mon 4/21/08	Thu 4/24/08
179	100%	✓	Routings	4 days	Mon 4/21/08	Thu 4/24/08
180	100%	✓	Vendor Master	4 days	Mon 4/21/08	Thu 4/24/08
181	100%	✓	Purchasing Info Records	4 days	Mon 4/21/08	Thu 4/24/08
182	100%	✓	Customer Master	4 days	Mon 4/21/08	Thu 4/24/08
183	100%	✓	Customer Credit Limit	4 days	Mon 4/21/08	Thu 4/24/08
184	100%	✓	Customer Material Infor Records	4 days	Mon 4/21/08	Thu 4/24/08
185	100%	✓	Freight Carriers	4 days	Mon 4/21/08	Thu 4/24/08
186	100%	✓	Pricing	4 days	Mon 4/21/08	Thu 4/24/08
187	100%	✓	GL Accounts	4 days	Mon 4/21/08	Thu 4/24/08
188	100%	✓	Cost Centers	4 days	Mon 4/21/08	Thu 4/24/08
189	100%	✓	Cost Elements	4 days	Mon 4/21/08	Thu 4/24/08
190	100%	✓	Profit Centers	4 days	Mon 4/21/08	Thu 4/24/08
191						
192						
193	**100%**	✓	⊟ **Cut-Over Phase**	**15 days?**	**Mon 4/14/08**	**Fri 5/2/08**
194	**100%**	✓	⊟ **Refine Production Support Plan**	**10 days?**	**Mon 4/14/08**	**Fri 4/25/08**
195	100%	✓	Create Post-Go-Live Issues Log	1 day?	Wed 4/23/08	Wed 4/23/08
196	100%	✓	Identify Team for Post-Go-Live Support	5 days	Mon 4/21/08	Fri 4/25/08
197	100%	✓	Create Cut-Over Plan	5 days	Mon 4/14/08	Fri 4/18/08
198	**100%**	✓	⊟ **Refine Cut-Over Plan**	**5 days?**	**Mon 4/14/08**	**Fri 4/18/08**
199	100%	✓	Review Conversion Timing	5 days	Mon 4/14/08	Fri 4/18/08
200	100%	✓	Communicate Timing to Business	1 day?	Mon 4/14/08	Mon 4/14/08

Task # 175 - # 190, Extend Master Data in PRD: It is time to extend or load master data into the SAP production system. This is master data only. No transactions can be processed prior to appropriate time in the cutover plan. The master data is also validated at this time to ensure that we migrated all of the appropriate master data. If this was not done properly, it will cause problems during the open data load during cutover. Therefore, it is a good idea to check the open data records to make sure that you have the appropriate master data in the system that the open loads are dependent on.

Task # 193 - # 200, Cut-over Phase: This is the beginning of the cut-over phase. Here we ensure that the production support plan is in place. Also make sure that there is a Post – Go-Live issues log ready and the team is set up to provide support. Ensure the cut-over plan has the appropriate level of detail and that the steps in the cut-over plan are in the proper sequence. Included in this section is a reminder to communicate the timing of the down-time for the new site and the timing of the cut-over to the entire company. Over communication is not possible.

Task # 202 - # 226, The Cut-Over Plan: This is not the real cutover plan, but more of a place holder. The detailed cutover plan is covered in Chapter 11 "The Cut-over Plan".

The project plan is a critical tool to a successful implementation. It is extremely important to follow the plan and diligently keep the plan updated with the latest status. The project manager needs to stay a couple of steps ahead. Without a project plan there would be no way for a project manager to do this. Without a project plan it would be very difficult to measure the project's success against the timeline. It would also be difficult to keep the team focused on the proper activities.

I encourage you to use this plan. Take it, make it your own. Modify it to suite your projects and enjoy the success.

Figure 5.10 Sample Project Plan (tasks 202 –226)

ID	% Work Complete		Task Name	Duration	Start	Finish
202	100%		The Cut-Over Plan	6 days	Fri 4/25/08	Fri 5/2/08
203	0%		12 Noon Stop transactions - Lock users out	0 days	Fri 4/25/08	Fri 4/25/08
204	0%		1PM Enter SOs, POs, and Inventory Data from 06	0 days	Fri 4/25/08	Fri 4/25/08
205	100%		Begin Finance Close - 06	3 days	Fri 4/25/08	Mon 4/28/08
206	0%		Load Purchase Orders	0 days	Fri 4/25/08	Fri 4/25/08
207	100%		Load Sales Orders	5 days	Fri 4/25/08	Wed 4/30/08
208	0%		Complete Finance Month Close - Company Code 06	0 days	Fri 4/25/08	Fri 4/25/08
209	0%		Run FI Extracts	0 days	Fri 4/25/08	Fri 4/25/08
210	100%		Early Friday AM Extract Open AR, AP, and GL from pcMRP	1 day	Fri 4/25/08	Fri 4/25/08
211						
212	0%		Open Loads	0 days	Sat 4/26/08	Sat 4/26/08
213	0%		Inactivate/activate auto-posting for reconciliation accounts	0 days	Sat 4/26/08	Sat 4/26/08
214	0%		Inventory Balances	0 days	Sat 4/26/08	Sat 4/26/08
215	0%		Year to date GL Balances	0 days	Sat 4/26/08	Sat 4/26/08
216	0%		Open AR Balances	0 days	Sat 4/26/08	Sat 4/26/08
217	0%		Open AP Balances	0 days	Sat 4/26/08	Sat 4/26/08
218						
219						
220	100%		Final Data Validation	0.5 days	Mon 4/28/08	Mon 4/28/08
221						
222	0%		Go-Live	0 days	Tue 4/29/08	Tue 4/29/08
223						
224	0%		Post Go-Live Tasks	0 days	Fri 5/2/08	Fri 5/2/08
225	0%		Create Planning File	0 days	Fri 5/2/08	Fri 5/2/08
226	0%		Run MRP	0 days	Fri 5/2/08	Fri 5/2/08

Chapter 6
The Project Environment

"Enthusiasm releases the drive to carry you over obstacles and adds significance to all you do."
– Norman Vincent Peale

Let's start by checking the attitude at the door. The most important thing in a high stress project such as an SAP implementation is to keep a positive attitude and do your best to promote the attitude that anything can be accomplished if you put your mind to it.

Much of the job of a project manager is keeping the team upbeat in an effort to maintain the tempo of the project. You need to be a good conductor to keep each of the instruments in an orchestra work together to make beautiful music.

You have to address your team members' concerns quickly and thoroughly. If you don't, they will waste time and bring down the moral of the team. They will begin to make noise that sound nothing like a great musical accompaniment from John Williams. Share the plan with them early and let them question the plan. You will hear this repeated way too many times, but it needs to be pointed out each time it is applied to enforce its' importance. Communication is critical for a successful SAP implementation. If you approach a project with a positive attitude, you will have more control over the environment than you think.

In addition to the emotional environment, there are

several aspects of the physical environment that need to be considered.

The War Room also known as the Team Room is a room dedicated to the project. Often it is a conference room that has been dedicated to the project throughout the duration of the implementation. Ideally it should be separate from the Training Room, but depending on the size of the facility, one room can sometimes double for both. It is amazing how many times I have had to go to battle with plant managers to get a dedicated room for a couple of months to serve as the war room.

There is so much activity going on during an implementation and so many people will be utilizing the room for what should be _the_ most important activity going on at the plant during these two months that there absolutely must be a dedicated room. This is the room where we complete the system configuration, perform unit tests and integration tests, hold daily status meetings, hold countless business process integration discussions and is often where we end up eating one or two meals a day. A dedicated room allows the project team to stay out of the way of the day-to-day business at the plant and it allows the team members (including the key users from the plant) to get away from their day-to-day jobs to focus on the project.

In most cases, the war room has been located in an area of the building or campus that is out of the way. This is generally a good thing. It keeps people from poking their heads in and disturbing the team. People must make a purposeful trip to the room if it is in a remote area.

During one of my implementations in Puerto Rico, the plant manager converted a storage room into the war room. It was located behind the production floor, on the opposite end of the building to the office workers. It was about a three to four minute walk to the offices. The worst part was that the roof in this storage room leaked – in several places. In Puerto Rico, it rained on us every day. At about 1:30PM every day, the water would start flowing down the walls and drops of water would fall in several places throughout the room. We would have to slide our laptops over to avoid getting them wet and we strategically placed plastic trash cans throughout the room to collect the falling water. We felt a little unwelcome in that plant to say the least. I was told that they fixed the leaky roof as soon as we left so they could make better use of the room that they had cleared out for us. We were not upset about the leaky roof. We always look back on it and have a good laugh. It was in some ways a bit of a team builder. I always look back on implementations with fond memories – even when we were all wet.

I think it is important to keep snacks in the room. It helps people to keep energized and snack food can help keep the mood light and fun.

As I mentioned in Chapter 3 "Project Preparation", the war room will need plenty of network connections (which can usually be handled by adding a couple of network switches or hubs in the room itself). In fact, I often carried little 4 or 5 port switch in my briefcase. The room should also have PCs for the champions and key users to use for testing and for sharing data. A few USB flash drives always come in handy (if the use of flash drives is not against your company policy). The room should also have a dry erase board for sharing ideas, brain storming and making activity status exposed or public. It is a good idea to have a printer in the room, but not absolutely needed if there is a printer nearby.

The training room must have a projector and a dry ease board. It also must have at least 1 PC for every 2 trainees. Ideally each person should have their own PC during the training. Hands-on training is best therefore the training will run faster if each person has their own PC. The training room should also have a printer because it is important for people to see the outputs that will be printed during each business process procedure they are being trained on. There should be enough room next to each PC to have some space for training documents and note taking. I like to place the PCs under the desks or tables and only have monitors, keyboards and mice on the surface of the desks or tables. This allows more room for note taking and it is easier for the trainee to see the presentation or whiteboard over the tops of the monitors.

The Post-Project Environment

After the project is complete, the SAP Team will still have a lot of collaborative work to do. They will need to support post go-live issues and they will be working together on enhancements. The SAP team should be together in one area and not spread throughout the building. At one company, they asked the SAP team members to sit in the departments that they supported. This may me a good idea for the first week or two after go-live, but I do not recommend this as a permanent working environment. The SAP team should sit together so they can lean on each other for support. SAP is a cross-functional application. All of the modules are connected together and people need to communicate with each other about the interconnectivity on a regular basis.

The areas in which they work should promote collaboration. If they are in cubicles, the walls should be short enough for them to see over while they are sitting down so they can quickly ask each other questions. They can also be in a room together with no cubicles, just desks. These environments work very well for SAP teams.

I worked at a company that had high cubicles for all of their office workers. I asked the plant manager to replace my team's cubicle walls with shorter ones. When my SAP team found out they were the only ones in the building with short cubicle walls, they were a little upset. Let's just say that I was not the most popular manager in the plant. The people on the team felt exposed and they felt their privacy had been taken away. But over time they learned to appreciate their collaborative environment. I think the SAP team ended up having more fun, and being a more tight-knit department than any other. Because they could collaborate easily over several cubicle walls, they got more done in less time. They were extremely efficient. I think that transparency is important for an IT organization. The projects that they are working on and the status of those projects should be exposed to the entire organization. Lower cubicle walls added to the department transparency and increased effective communication.

Chapter 7
The Configuration Phase

"A man who dares to waste one hour of time has not discovered the value of life."

– Charles Darwin

The SMART Approach to implementing SAP allows two weeks for the configuration and unit testing of new sites in SAP R/3 or ECC. This may seem like a very short time, but in fact it is plenty of time. Remember, we are not configuring the system from scratch. We don't have to worry about the detailed baseline configuration such as order types, item categories, pricing procedures, output procedures, etc. All we really need to configure are the parts of IMG (the SAP configuration menu) that are specific to a new site. This is because, by design, we want the new company to follow the same business processes that the rest of the company uses. We only need to consider configuration additions that are needed for the new site to operate in SAP.

The "AS-IS" Processes

Most SAP implementations start by performing a detailed analysis of the "AS-IS" business processes. This study is designed to ensure that all of the processes for running the business have been considered. In order to have a successful implementation, you must uncover and study these "AS-IS" processes and map them to the "TO-BE" business processes. This exercise can take a few months in a normal SAP implementation. Especially when companies do not already have well-documented business processes.

The TO-BE Processes

In the SMART Approach, we save a lot of time by almost skipping the "AS-IS" business process analysis. We use the System Integration Questionnaire to discover how the company is set up. It gives us clues, showing us where to look for major differences between the global business processes and those of the new site. But for the most part, we don't care what business process they are currently running. As my teenage daughter would say, "OMG! What do you mean you don't care!" I know it is harsh to say it in such a blunt way, and I would never be so rude to people at the new site, but the reality is that we want to keep a consistent set of business processes throughout the entire company. We want to roll out our existing business processes. Therefore, we need to test to ensure that our standard corporate-sponsored processes will work in their business. If they believe that the standard process for a given business area will not work, it is up to them to prove it to us. They need to explain to us why the global process will not achieve the objective.

The Exceptions

There are exceptions to every rule. Although we set aside two weeks for configuration and unit testing, you will find that some additional configuration will be needed throughout the project. During testing, you may uncover things that require minor fixes or adjustments for things that come up in business process discussions which happen throughout the project. Most of these discussions get deep during integration testing and training because it is not until that time when the folks from the new site see the global processes operating in the SAP environment.

For each major process difference, we review the options and come up with a quick decision on how to handle it. Assuming that we do not have a process that handles the scenario already configured in SAP, there are certain rules of thumb I apply to these exceptions. First, we have to determine if the process is currently handled within their ERP or if it is managed manually or by other mini applications or databases. My experience has been that most companies have several applications and databases that they use for different parts of the business. If a process does not touch the core ERP already, then we may not have to add it to SAP during this short implementation. In these cases, we will let them continue to use their existing process. Since it is my charter to make the most use out of our existing investment in SAP, eventually we will come back and replace those mini applications and database with a SAP NetWeaver solution at a later time. If a process is partially handled in their ERP, or use reports generated from their ERP, we will show them equivalent reports from ECC or SAP BI.

Once in a while we will come across a company that has a more elaborate process for a particular part of their business. For example, they may handle returns processing for another company or they could require configurable sales orders instead of standard orders. As we grow, we add new business process to our portfolio in SAP. When we acquire another company, we then have a portfolio of business process offerings for them.

Usually they can find a process within our portfolio that will work in their business model. Occasionally we will find that the newly acquired business runs a better process than we do. However, during the project, we ask them to run our corporate-sponsored process anyway – for the sake of time. After the project is complete we will go back and roll out that better process to the rest of the sites that are already on our single global instance of SAP.

It is possible that a newly acquired company is located in a country where we have not done business before. Some countries have laws that need to be considered when implementing a system. My reference to our implementation in Brazil in Chapter 3 is a perfect example of this. We had to add Brazilian localization configuration. Knowing this upfront, I added an additional month to our standard implementation timeframe. We completed the implementation in Brazil in 3 months rather than 2 months. A three month implementation with Brazilian localization configuration is still quite an accomplishment. We used our standard configuration where we could and added the Brazilian localization where necessary.

The key is to start with a baseline configuration for your major processes such as Order-to-Cash and Procure-to-Pay. Use this baseline as the cookie-cutter and do your very best to roll this cookie-cutter approach out to all of your sites. Doing this will make your entire organization much more agile, and efficient.

Chapter 8
User Acceptance Testing

"Vision is perhaps our greatest strength. It makes us peer into the future and lends shape to the unknown."

– Li Ka Shing

User acceptance testing is arguably the most important activity in the entire project. It runs neck-in-neck with the data migration activities in the race for most critical phase in a successful implementation.

As I mentioned earlier, User Acceptance testing, which is often synonymous with Integration Testing is often the first chance the key users get to touch the system and start to learn how to use SAP. They are often excited, very curious, and sometimes skeptical. This is when the questions get detailed and you can almost see the cogs in the wheels of their minds turning. They are often enlightened and delighted with the power and versatility that SAP offers. They are delighted that the constraints of their legacy systems will not exist in SAP. (Of course SAP has its' own constraints and those will be exposed here as well.) By far, most people that I have moved to SAP absolutely love it compared to their legacy systems.

To prepare for Integration Testing, the BSAs start with the standard test scripts, and update them with details for the new site. They add data to the test scripts that make the testing run smooth. Materials or part numbers, customers, and vendors which will be used for testing are added to the test scripts. Below you will find the standard set processes and scenarios covered by test scripts that are typically used when rolling out SAP to a new manufacturing plant.

- Master Data Maintenance
  - o Material Masters
  - o Bills of Material
  - o Customer Masters
  - o Vendor Masters
  - o Approved Vendor List
- Forecast Process
- Procurement Process
- Receiving Process
- Accounts Payable Process
- Incoming Inspection Process
- Inventory Management Process
- Production Planning & Control Process
- Finance & Controlling Process
- Finished Goods Process
  - o Settlement
- Sales & Shipping Process
  - o Standard Order Scenario
  - o Free / Sample Order Scenario
- Accounts Receivable Process
  - o Credit Memo Scenario
  - o Debit Memo Scenario
  - o Customer Credit Management
  - o Dynamic Credit Hold Scenario
- RMA (Return Material Authorization) Process
  - o Return for Credit Scenario
  - o Repair / Replace Scenario
- Return to Vendor Process
- Physical Inventory Process
- Month End Process
- System Background Job Processing

To show the level of detail of the integration test scripts, see figures 8.1 through 8.4 which are images of a completed integration test script.

Figure 8.1   Sample Integration Test Script

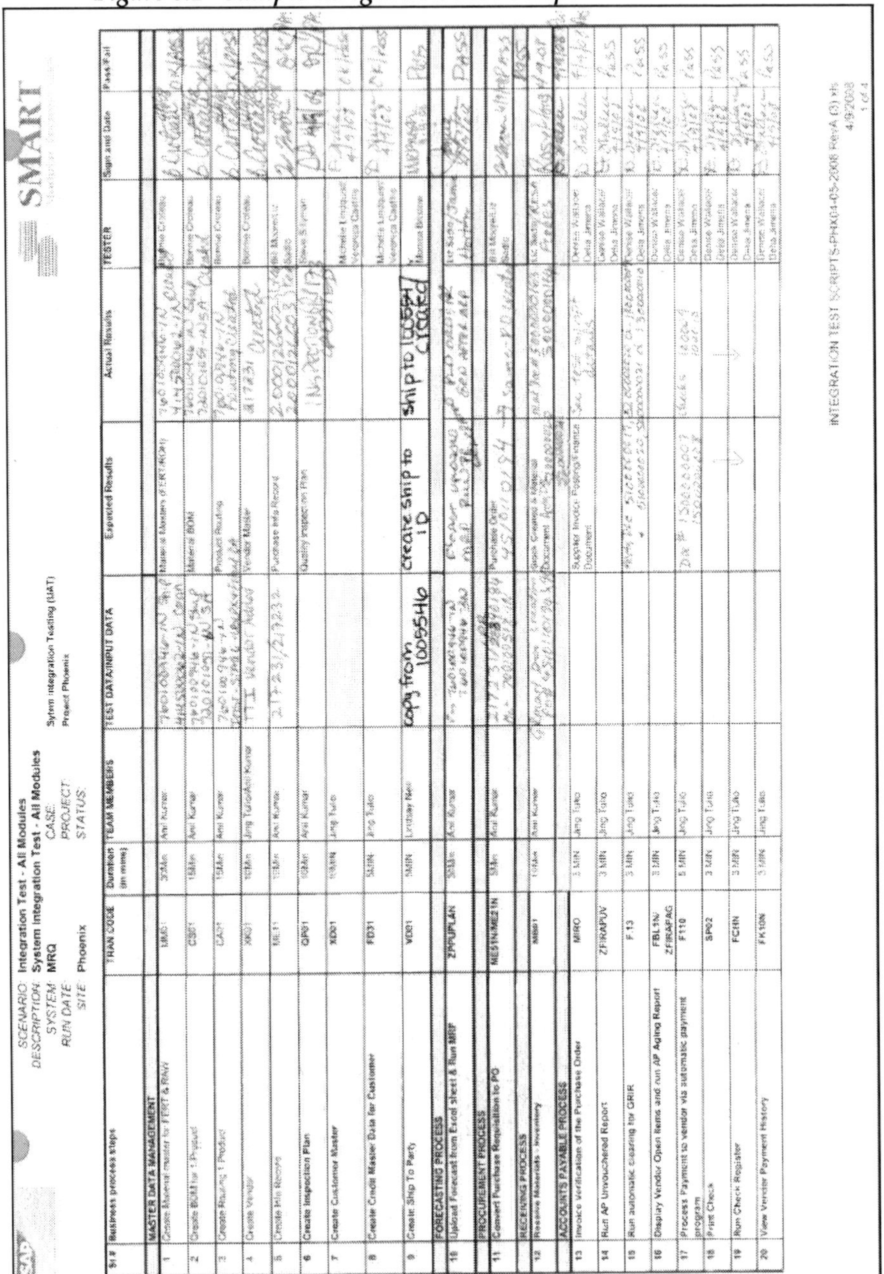

Figure 8.2 Sample Integration Test Script

Figure 8.3 Sample Integration Test Script

Figure 8.4   Sample Integration Test Script

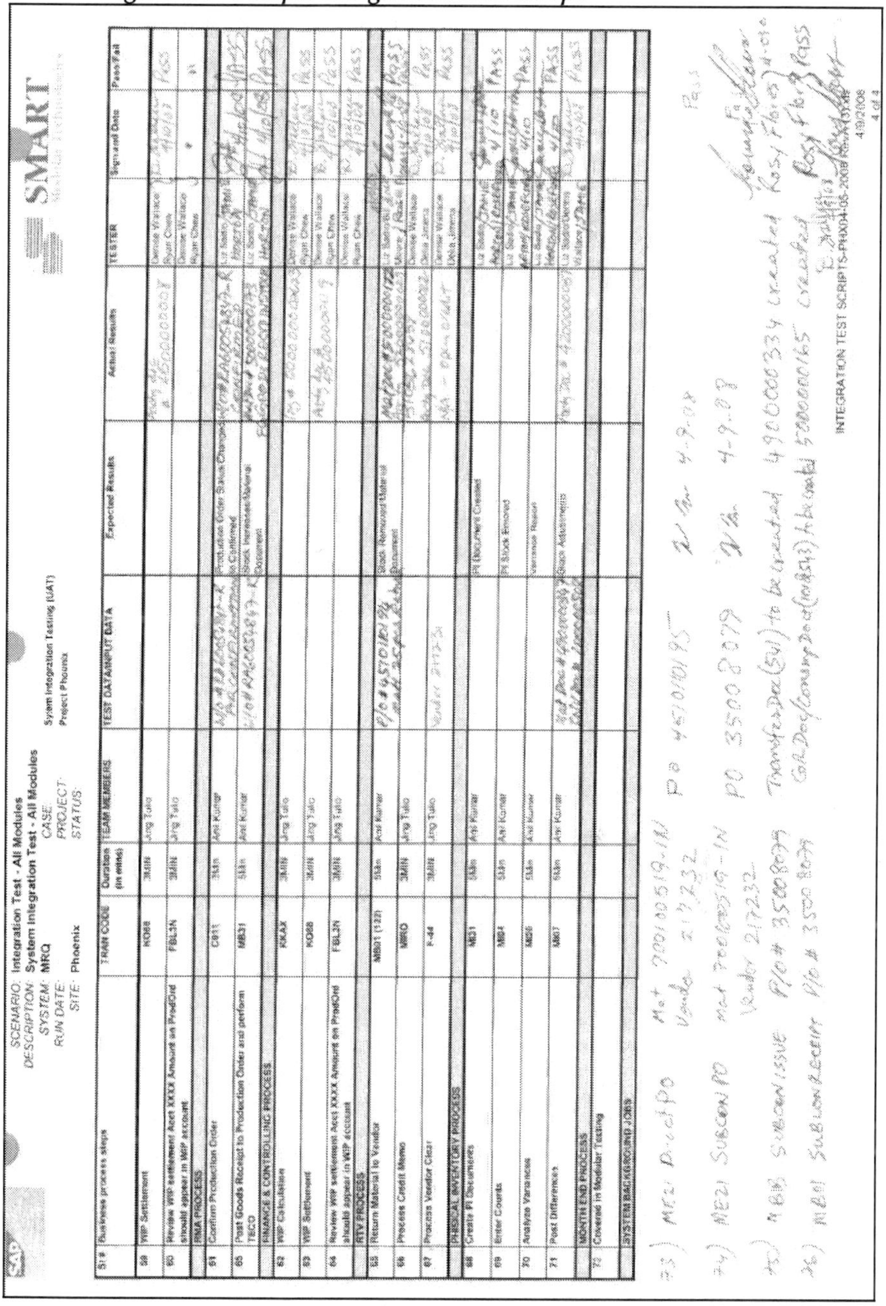

You will notice that each step of the test script is signed and dated by the tester. This is not only a best practice, but it is important to maintain SOX compliance. The BSAs are responsible for getting each step signed-off. If a problem is uncovered during testing, the problem is noted by the key user or champion on the test script and it is recorded by the BSA on the issues log. The BSAs fix any configuration problems as soon as possible and have the users test the functionality again. Configuration fixes are usually ready for testing in the QA system by the following day. At worst case, they must be ready for the final round of integration testing which happens in the second week of testing.

Over the years our standard set of integration test scripts has migrated from a series of independent business process test scripts to a few test script files containing a full suite of business processes. There should also be test scenarios that cover negative testing to ensure that the configuration that was maintained for the new plant did not negatively impact other manufacturing plants which also use the global baseline configuration.

I think it is up to each team how they structure the integration test scripts, as long as they cover all of the business processes and all of the appropriate scenarios.

Integration Test Schedule

When using the SMART Approach to implementing SAP, you should conduct the integration testing in the war room over a period of a couple of days. In order to complete the integration testing quickly, it has to be well coordinated. Make sure that all of the parties are in the room at the right time. The champions from the sister site will often have to fly to the new site so the travel schedule has to be in line with the integration testing and training schedules.

Figure 8.5 shows a sample integration test schedule. Each step of an integration test is numbered and the schedule shows the step number, the time that the step is to take place on a given day, the BSA who is responsible for the configuration for that step, the champion from the sister site who will be assisting the key user, and the key user who will be performing that step of the test.

The project manager usually acts as a coordinator during the integration testing. They need to make sure everyone is in the room at the right time.

Figure 8.5 Sample Integration Test Schedule

SI	TIME Wednesday	BSA	SMART Champion	ADTRON Key User		SI	TIME Thursday	BSA	SMART Champion	ADTRON Key User
1-4	9-10:30	Anil/Jing	Louisa C.	Bonnie Croteau		33-34	9:00-9:15	Anil	Bryan	Rosa/Briana/Liz
5	10:30-10:45	Anil	Jennifer M.	Bill Moore/Liz		35-37	9:15-9:30	Jing	Ryan C.	Denise
6	10:45-11:00	Anil		Steve Sillyman		38-40	9:30-9:40	Lindsay	Katie P.	Monica
7-8	11:00-11:15	Jing	Veronica C.	Michelle		41	9:40-9:50	Jing	Veronica C.	Michelle
9	11:15-11:25	Lindsay	Katie P.	Monica Bristow		42-48	9:50-10:15	Lindsay	Indy B.	Rosa
10-11	11:30-12:00	Anil	Bryan S.	Jamie/Liz		49-50	10:15-10:25	Jing	Ryan C.	Denise
12	1:30-1:40	Anil	Bryan S.	Bill/Liz		51-53	10:30-10:45	Jing	Veronica C.	Michelle
13	1:40-1:55	Anil	Gopal K.	Rosa/Briana/Liz		54	10:45-10:50	Lindsay	Katie P.	Monica
14-21	2:00-2:30	Jing	Delia J.	Denise Wallace		55-57	10:50-11:00	Lindsay	Indy B.	Rosa
22	2:30-2:40	Jing	Anne G.	Denise		58	11:00-11:10	Anil	Gopal K.	Rosa/Briana/Liz
23	2:40-2:45	Anil		Steve Sillyman		59	11:10-11:15	Lindsay	Indy B.	Rosa
24-25	2:45-3:00	Anil	Gopal K.	Rosa/Liz		60	11:15-11:25	Anil	Gopal K.	Rosa/Briana/Liz
26-28	3:00-3:15	Anil	Bryan S.	Jamie/Liz		61-63	11:25-11:30	Jing	Ryan C.	Denise
29	3:15-3:25	Anil	Gopal K.	Rosa/Briana/Liz		64-65	11:30-11:45	Anil	Gopal K.	Rosa/Briana/Liz
30-32	3:25-4:00	Jing	Ryan C.	Denise		66-68	1:30-1:45	Jing	Ryan	Denise
						69	1:50-2:00	Anil	Jennifer M.	Bill/Liz
						70-71	2:00-2:15	Jing	Delia	Denise
						72-74	2:15-2:30	Anil	Gopal K.	Rosa/Briana/Liz
						75	2:30-2:45	Jing	Ryan	Denise

At the beginning of the project, the project manager should make sure that the managers approve time for the champions and key users to perform the testing.

During the days of testing in the war room, the project manager needs to be looking a few steps ahead to make sure that the right people are in the room at the right time to perform their portion of the tests. By definition, the integration tests must be performed in the order that business transactions would normally be performed. If someone is not available, it can cause a chain reaction that delays the completion of the testing. It wastes the time of the people who are waiting to perform their steps. Ultimately it is the project manager's responsibility to ensure that each test script is tested and signed-off by the business stake holders.

Chapter 9
Change Management & Training

"Anyone who stops learning is old, whether at twenty or eighty. Anyone who keeps learning stays young. The greatest thing in life is to keep your mind young."

– Henry Ford

The larger the organization, the more change management will be required. Change management, in this case, is simply preparing the organization for the impending SAP implementation. Training is a component of change management. There are several means of communication that you should take advantage of to prepare the site for the new business processes and systems they will be using. Posters in break rooms, meetings, frequent status updates and announcements are all important change management tools.

A major component of change management is the training strategy. The strategy will differ depending on the number of people that need to be trained, where the students are geographically, number of trainers available, and the time available for training. If employees are geographically dispersed and it is not practical to bring them all together for the appropriate training sessions, the strategy will need to include remote training options.

Training is something that is technically done throughout

the project. It starts as we discuss the standard corporate business processes. The key users get trained during the integration testing. But the masses will be trained in the last two weeks of the project. It is best to wait until the very end of the project to perform training because if you train people too early, they will forget what they have learned before go-live. Therefore, we always schedule training during the final two weeks of the project. Sometimes if the project timeline slips, we end up combining the last week of integration testing with the first week of training. You can only do this if the team performing the training is separate from the team performing the testing. This also only works if you implement a standard global footprint and therefore the testing is merely to confirm that the new organizational configuration is working properly and we are not introducing a significant amount of new functionality or new processes which people will need to be trained on.

We use BPPs, (Business Process Procedures) as training documents. BPPs are a well-know component of the ASAP methodology. It is very important to follow the training materials during the training because we want the users to refer back to the BPPs if they have questions about the processes before they call for help. If they are familiar with the BPPs, they will know that they can use the BPPs as reference materials.

Although the key users have only been exposed SAP a week or two longer than the rest of the users, we ask that they help in the training. The champions are the ones who run the classes and lead the training. The appropriate SAP team member also sits in on the training sessions, but they are only there as support. The reason for this structure is that it mimics the support structure. We find that people are likely to go to the ones they learned from for help. If the SAP team performs the training, they are likely to get the support calls that a champion user or a key user is capable of answering. The SAP team's time is better spent preparing for the next project, adding new functionality to the SAP environment, or rolling out SAP to another site.

The training schedule should be communicated early. This gives people enough time to plan to attend the training sessions. It is imperative that the appropriate people attend the training sessions because there will not be enough time in a fast implementation to perform training again before go-live.

Over time companies can create training tutorials and post them on their intranet sites. These tutorials are great for refreshers that people can refer to after go-live. The tutorials are also useful for new employees to review to gain an understanding of how to process transactions in SAP.

All training materials should be maintained on the company's intranet site for people to access anytime. During training classes, instructors should show people where to access these materials. The materials should include the process overview presentations, BPPs, tips and tricks, FAQs, on-line tutorials, and cue cards (quick cheat sheets or quick reference guides).

Please do not underestimate the training efforts. Someone should be appointed to ensure training materials are available, training facilities are sufficient, trainers are available, the training plan and schedule is developed and communicated. This can be very challenging, but never impossible.

Chapter 10
Data Migration

"When you feel like giving up, remember why you held on for so long in the first place."

– Anonymous

Data Migration is the most time-consuming activity in the project. It is also one of the most critical activities in the project. Issues that arise during data migration could delay the project. It is imperative to start this activity very early. Data migration is an activity where there is so much going on that it is easy to make mistakes even if you are very careful.

Earlier in this book, the differences between master data and open data and the timing of the data loads were detailed. The data migration is usually the most challenging part of the implementation. It is critical to get the appropriate data loaded prior to go-live. Data migration is difficult because some data elements rely on other data elements meaning that some data must be loaded prior to other data. There are dependencies between data objects and even dependencies from field to field within a single data object.

Extracting the appropriate data from the legacy systems is challenging as well because often the legacy system experts have not needed to provide such complete sets of data in the past. They need to know what data is important to extract. SAP absolutely requires certain fields in order to process transactions, so we must ensure we at least have data to load into those required fields.

Once the data is extracted, it must be loaded correctly. There are many considerations when loading the data. Every field from the legacy system has to be mapped to the appropriate field in SAP. Much of the data does not map directly from one field to another. Much of the data needs to be transformed. For example, the number "7" in a legacy system may denote consigned materials. In the SAP Sales and Distribution module, "K" denotes a consigned material. Therefore, the data migration maps will show "7 = K" for that field in the map. The data migration maps have to include the translation rules for each field in addition to the name of each legacy field as it is mapped to the technical SAP field names. The maps also include field descriptions to help determine the use of the fields. Some fields will require a default value to be maintained. The default values for each of these fields must also be maintained in the data migration maps. Default values are used when the legacy system does not have an entry for a field that is required in SAP. Default values are also used in fields requiring organizational data such as the company code, plant ID, sales organization, etc.

The BSAs are responsible for the data migration maps. They work with the people extracting the data from the legacy system to ensure that we get all of the data required for the load. The BSA then work with the data migration expert to ensure that the fields map properly in SAP.

Data migration templates are required for all data objects which will need to be loaded via a program. This is a given because the programs need to take into consideration the rules that are outlined in the maps. It is also a good practice to create data migration templates for the master data that will be entered by hand. This will help avoid confusion when entering the master data. Plus it is important to have considered all scenarios when creating data migration maps.

The material master is one of the most complex data objects. It is also a place where it is easy to create unnecessary duplicates when loading materials for new plants. To avoid

Figure 10.1   Sample Data Migration Map (Material Master)

SAP Field	MATNR	MAKTX	MEINS	MATKL	BISMT	BRGEW
SAP Description	Material	Material Description	Base Unit of Measure	Material Group	Legacy Material	Gross Weight
Legacy System Field	tcibd001.item	tcibd001.dsca	tcibd001.cuni	tcibd001.citg	*tcibd001.dfit	*tcibd001.wght
Field Description	Item	Description	Inventory Unit	Item Group	*Derived from Item	Weight
Programming Notes	ok	ok	ok	See Change/Comments	DO NOT USE	Defaults to 0.1

* Clarification required for mapping

Changes:
1. Until new Material Groups are entered in SAP, use Item Group mapped against Sister Site's current Material Groups.
2. New Material Groups will be equivalent to World Wide Commodity Codes which are already in place in the legacy system.

This illustration only represents part of the map. If you were looking at the actual spreadsheet, it extends to the right horizontally covering every field in the material master.

this, we have component engineers review the component materials from the new site. They map the components from the new site to the components we already have in SAP. If the materials already exist in SAP, instead of loading duplicate materials, we extend the materials from the plant of record to the new plant. The rest of the components will need to be loaded. This is not an easy task. Usually the part numbers are not the same, the component engineers have to manually compare the material descriptions or supplier part numbers to those in SAP. But this is a very important step. If this is not done the company will not be able to take advantage of synergies between plants that use the same set of materials in their BOMs (Bill of Materials). They will not have inventory visibility between plants. If the plants share the same component part numbers, and one plant has components in inventory that another plant needs, they can perform a plant-to-plant transfer instead of ordering new materials from the vendors. Companies also gain pricing advantages from vendors when multiple plants use the same components. If each plant uses different part numbers, the company could lose this visibility and miss out on volume pricing agreements with their vendors.

Eventually you will end up with so many part numbers in your system your engineers will have problems selecting materials for new BOMs.

This also points out the importance of using the same vendor IDs in each of the manufacturing plants globally. By extending existing vendors to the new plant, it is easier to administer global volume pricing agreements with the vendors. It is also easier to maintain the AVL (Approved Vendors List) for each component.

If customers are common between plants, extending the customer IDs to the new plant for the shared customers allows the company to show a single face to their customers. Reporting can be combined and customer satisfaction is increased.

Each data object should be compared for synergies that can be gained by the organization.

Chapter 11
The Cut-Over Plan

"Cowards die many times before their deaths; the valiant never taste of death but once."

– William Shakespeare

The cut-over is when the project really gets exciting. Some say it is really exciting to see a good plan come together. But I think it's more exciting to see a good plan being well executed. In this chapter, I will discuss the building of the cut-over plan as well as the execution of that plan.

The cut-over plan is much more crucial than the project plan. The project plan needs to be followed and updated weekly and sometimes daily. If some tasks are not timed exactly right, there is usually time to catch up – even in a 2 month project plan. A cut-over plan, on the other hand, is followed daily and sometimes hourly. I have even seen sections split into 15 minute segments. There is not much room for error or slippage. There is very little room to catch up if you fall behind. It is very important for the project manager to constantly be following and updating the status of each step on the cut-over plan.

In the example below, you will see references to MRP & MBP. These are system names for SAP R/3 or ECC and SAP BI production systems. We generally rollout these systems to a new site at the same time. During this time we also implement

SAP GRC (Governance, Risk & Compliance) as well.

Generally speaking, whichever applications are needed for the global processes are implemented at the same time. However, the more applications the company uses, the more complex the implementation will be; the more complex the hardware landscape will be; and the more resources you will need to implement and maintain the applications and servers. I highly recommend keeping your SAP landscape as simple as possible. There are always multiple ways of accommodating business processes in SAP applications. If a process can be handled in ECC or one of the other SAP NetWeaver applications that you already have, you should make use of these existing applications instead of implementing a new application. This is obviously the economical approach. Not only will you save money on purchase of the software and the annual maintenance, but you will also need fewer people to maintain your environment and there will be fewer servers to maintain. You will also save time rolling out your global footprint to all of your locations.

The Anatomy of a Cut-over Plan

I always use a spreadsheet or actually workbook to build the cut-over plan. The first tab contains the entire plan. Another tab is used as a subset of the plan for activities that are performed on a weekend. I call this tab the "Weekend Warriors" tab and use it in a presentation to the people who will be involved during the cutover weekend, their managers, and the senior managers at the site undergoing the implementation. This presentation is given to show the activities the team will be performing over the weekend and to ensure the users will be available over the weekend to perform their steps.

Cut-over Plan

This tab of the workbook contains the extremely detailed cut-over plan. The plan contains columns for the step number, prerequisites, date, day, start time, end time, area of responsibility, person responsible, status, activity, and remarks or comments.

The step number is important because in a cut-over plan, it is often very important to perform the steps in a certain sequence. The "Prerequisite" column notes the step number that absolutely must be performed prior to this step. The date is simply the date that the step is to be performed. The day represents the day of the week that the step is to be performed. It is not necessary, but helps as a reference. The "From (Time)" notes when the step is to start. The "To (Time)" shows when the step is to be completed, which is important when referencing prerequisites. "Area" is used for either SAP module or business department responsible for the step. "Person Responsible" shows the name of the person or people who will actually be performing the step. The "Status" column is for the project manager to note the completion of each step. "Activity" is the description of the task. The "Remarks" or "Comments" column can hold information that is either important for that step or the results from that step.

Cut-over activities generally start about 2 weeks prior to go-live. The cut-over always happens over a financial period closing. This is to ensure the books are closed in the legacy system and all transactions from the new fiscal period occur in the new SAP system.

Figure 11.1 Sample Cut-over Plan (steps 1 – 8)

Step	Pre	Date	Day	From (Time)	To (Time)	Area	Who	Status	Activity Description	Remarks
1.0		04/11/08	Friday	8:00 AM		IT	Amy		SAP Logon Pad Rollout Confirmation	1 week
2.0		04/11/08	Friday	6:00 PM		All	All Business		**Integration Test + Functional Test Sign-off**	
3.0		04/11/08	Friday	8:00 AM	5:00 PM	All	SAP Team		**Extract Master Data + Prepare for Upload**	
									** Cut-Off for Master Data Entry in PC MRP **	
3.1						SD	Amy		Customer Master	
3.2						SD	Amy		Customer Credit Limits	
3.3						MM	Amy		Vendor Master	
3.4						PP	Amy		Material Master	
3.5						PP	Amy		BOMs	
3.6						MM	Amy		AVL	
4.0		4/18/2008 Friday / 4/23/2008 Wednesday		8:00:00 AM	8:00:00 AM				**Finish Master Data File Preparations & Sign-off for Upload**	
4.1						SD	Laks / Monica / Lindsay		Customer Master (Gloria)	
4.2						SD	Laks / Monica / Lindsay		Customer Credit Limits (Gloria)	
4.3						MM	Laks / Amy / Anil		Vendor Master (Gloria / Jamie)	
4.4						PP	Laks / Amy / Anil		Work Centers (Jamie)	
4.5						PP	Laks / Bonnie / Anil		Routings (Jamie)	
4.6						PP	Amy / Bonnie / Anil		Material Master (Jamie)	
4.7						PP	Amy / Bonnie / Anil		BOMs (Jamie)	
4.8						MM	Amy / Bill / Anil		AVL (Jamie)	
4.9						FI	Denise / Jing / Gloria		Fixed Asset Master & Balances (Gloria) - as of P6	
5.0		04/18/08	Friday	8:00 AM	6:00 PM	BASIS	Surendra G		**Printers setup in MRP & MBP**	
6.0		04/18/08	Friday		10:00 PM	IT	Amy		**Complete Extract Queries for Open Load**	
7.0		04/20/08	Sunday	12:00 PM	12:00 PM	BASIS	Ross		**Submit MRP Transport Req list**	
8.0	7.0	04/21/08	Monday	8:00 AM	12:00 PM	BASIS	Surendra G		**Transports to Production (MRP)**	
8.1		04/21/08	Monday	12:00 PM	4:00 PM	All	SAP Team		Validate Transports to Production	

Step # 1, SAP Logon Pad Rollout Confirmation: This is to ensure that all users will have access to SAP from their PCs. This step should be completed well before go-live.

Step # 2, Integration Test & Functional Test Sign-off: This is a place holder just to make sure that the testing is complete prior to starting the cut-over.

Step # 3, Master Data Extraction + Prepare for Upload: This is the cut-off for any master data that will be loaded in the SAP system. *It is important for the business to know that any master data they create in their legacy system from this point forward will need to be re-created in the SAP system manually.* During this step, each master data object that will be loaded via a program is extracted one last time from the legacy system. The data is formatted and transformed to work with the load programs by the SAP team. The rules from the data migration maps are applied. This process takes some time and must be complete prior to loading any open data. Therefore, start this activity two weeks before go-live. To ensure we keep track of all master data objects that will be loaded via a program, they are listed as sub steps (3.1 – 3.6 in this example).

Step # 4, Finish Master Data Preparation & Sign-off for Upload: Once the master data is formatted for load, it needs to be signed-off by the appropriate business managers prior to loading the data into the SAP production system. Each sub-step lists the managers responsible for signing-off on the data as well as the team members who are responsible for getting those signatures.

Step # 5, Printers setup: The printers must be created and tested at the SAP level as well as the operating system level. This activity should be complete at least a week before go-live.

Step # 6, Complete Extract Queries for Open Load: The cut-off for perfecting the open data extracts is also a week before go-live.

Step # 7, Submit Transport List for ECC: The list of transports generated from the configuration must be prioritized appropriately as not to cause errors when transported to the SAP production system. The BSAs maintain this transport list throughout the project to ensure that all of their configuration transports are represented and in the appropriate order on the transport list. Transport lists are required for SOX audits and are included in the project documentation. There are generally two lists that are maintained. One for transports required prior to data load, and one for transports to be moved after the data loads or final sign-off. It is a good practice to combine the transports for a project that are to be transported together into a single transport. The list must be submitted to the basis team prior to the first set of transports.

Step # 8, Transport to Production: The Basis person transports the configuration required prior to data load into the production environment. The BSAs then review the configuration in the SAP Production systems in step 8.1 to ensure that the configuration was transported properly and in the correct sequence. The configuration must be correct prior to loading master data.

Step # 10, Manual Configuration using FF Project User ID: Some configuration is not transportable. We actually have to go into the SAP Production system and configure the system manually. Each manually configured object is logged as a sub step to step 10 to ensure we do not forget to perform any of them. This configuration is done by checking out the Project User ID, so we know why it was done and because we use SAP GRC Fire Fighter functionality we can track who performed each step for audit purposes.

Step # 11, Create & Lock Users in SAP ECC & BI: At this time, the Basis person creates all of the new users in the SAP applications and ensures they have appropriate access rights in these systems. This is done using SAP GRC Access Enforcer to ensure that appropriate business managers approve the access for each of the new SAP users. However, all of the new users should not be able to transact in the system prior to go-live so all of the new user IDs are locked. Then unlock only the key users who will be helping with the data migration in sub step 11.1.

Figure 11.2 Sample Cut-over Plan (steps 9 – 14)

Step	Pre	Date	Day	From (Time)	To (Time)	Area	Who	Status	Activity Description	Remarks
9.0		04/21/08	Monday	4:00 PM	4:00 PM	BASIS	Surendra G		**Create User ID: PHOENIX in MRP/MBP**	
10.0		04/21/08	Monday	4:00 PM	7:00 PM	All	SAP Team		**Manual Configuration using FF: Phoenix**	
10.1						MM	Anil		Adtron Factory Calendar	
10.2						MM	Anil		Ensure MM Period is open for Period 8	
10.3						MM	Anil		Print Condition Master Data	
10.4						MM	Anil		Pick List Printer	
10.4						FI	Jing		Open Accounting Period for P6,P7,P8	
10.5						FI	Jing		Define number ranges	
10.6						FI	Jing		Copy Financial Statement Version to PCA	
10.7						FI	Jing		Create Check Lots	
10.8						FI	Jing		Create House Banks	
10.9						SD	Lindsay		Create Output Condition records	
11.0		04/22/08	Tuesday	8:00 AM		BASIS	Surendra G		**Create & lock users in MRP & MBP**	
11.1		04/22/08	Tuesday		5:00 PM	BASIS	Surendra G		**Release MRP User IDs for Key Users**	
12.0	10.0	04/23/08	Wednesday	8:00 AM	10:00 AM	FI	Jing / Denise /Gloria		**Master Data (Manual Entry & Validate) I**	
12.1						FI	Jing / Denise /Gloria		GL Accounts Master	
12.2						FI	Jing / Denise /Gloria		Cost Centers	
12.3						FI	Jing / Denise /Gloria		Profit Centers	
12.4						FI	Jing / Denise /Gloria		Fixed Asset Master & Balances as of P6	
13.0	4.0	04/23/08	Wednesday	10:00 AM		IT	Laks / Anil		**Master Data Upload & Validate**	
13.1						MM	Laks / Bonnie / Jamie		Material Master	
13.2						MM	Laks / Bonnie / Jamie		BOMs	
13.3						MM	Laks / Bill / Jamie		AVL	
13.4						PP	Laks / Bonnie / Jamie		Routings	
13.5						SD	Laks / Monica / Gloria		Customer Master	
13.6						SD	Laks / Monica / Gloria		Customer Credit Limit	
13.7		04/23/08	Wednesday		7:00 PM	IT	Laks / Denise / Bill / Jamie		Vendor Master	
14.0		04/24/08	Thursday	4:00 PM		All	All Business		*****STOP ALL Physical Material Processing*****	

Step # 12, Master Data (Manual Entry & Validate) I: All of the financial master data objects that were determined to be loaded manually are listed in sub steps of step 12. These are the financial master data objects that are required to be maintained prior to maintaining objects that are dependent on them. This financial master data will be used in the creation of other master data such as material masters, customer masters, and vendor masters. The key users manually enter this master data and then validate that the data is correct. This validation is captured to meet audit requirements.

Step # 13, Master Data Upload & Validate: All of the master data objects that were determined to be loaded via a program are listed in sub steps of step 13. This data is loaded and then manually reviewed and validated by the key users. Again, proof of this validation is documented to meet audit requirements.

Step # 14, Stop ALL Physical Material Processing: This step is not always required. In this example, the site that was undergoing the SAP implementation had a process whereby they transacted the physical material movements on the production floor and in the stock rooms on paper. Then a data entry clerk entered the transactions from the previous day in the legacy system. Therefore, the business managers at that site decided to stop all physical material movements on Thursday to make sure they were all entered into the legacy system by the end of day Friday - the last day of transactions in the legacy system.

Step # 15, Master Data (Manual Entry) II: These master data objects were determined to be loaded manually, but they were dependant on the master data that was loaded via program in step 13.

Step # 16, Submit transport list for BI: This is similar to Step # 7, but these transports are for the BI system rather than the ECC system. Once the transport list is confirmed to be correct, the BI configuration is transported to the BI production system and validated by the Business Systems Analysts on the SAP Team.

Figure 11.3 Sample Cut-over Plan (steps 15 – 23)

Step	Pre	Date	Day	From (Time)	To	(Time)	Area	Who	Status	Activity Description	Remarks
15.0		04/25/08	Friday	8:00 AM	6:00 PM		All	Adtron Champs		**Master Data (Manual Entry) II**	
15.1							PP	Bonnie		Work Centers	
15.2							PP	Bonnie		Batch Master ?? Verify w Mindie If Necessary	
15.3							QM	Steve		Inspection Characteristics	
15.4							QM	Steve		Inspection Plans	
16.0		04/25/08	Friday	1:30PM			BW	Gokul		Submit BW Transport Req list	
16.0		04/25/08	Friday	2:00 PM	5:00 PM		BASIS	Surendra G		**Transport to MBP**	
16.1		04/25/08	Friday	5:00 PM	7:00 PM		BW	Jing/ Gokul/ Indy		Cheking of transported objects/settings	
17.0		04/25/08	Friday	7:00 PM			BW	Gokul		Master Data Objects Loading in MBP	
18.0								Gokul/ Jing		Manual Configuration: - Update Cost Center Hierarchy 0COSTCENTER - Update Z_8KER file in ODS - Upload Master Data attribute for 0COMP_CODE - Verify master data tables for company code 06 (text and attributes) - Synchronization of A_PRCTR - Synchronization of 0COMPANY, A_COMPANY	
19.0		04/25/08	Friday	**Noon**			All	Amy		**STOP ALL TRANSACTIONS in PCMRP + Lock all users out (except FI)**	
19.1										**** Cut-Off for ALL System Activities in PCMRP ****	
20.0		04/25/08	Friday	Noon	2:00 PM		All	All Business		Complete all scheduled jobs (PCMRP)	
21.0	20.0	04/25/08	Friday	2:00 PM			FI	ALL Finance		**Begin FI Close**	
22.0		04/26/08	Saturday	8:00 AM			IT	All		Schedule Background Job/Process Chains in MRP & MBP	
23.0		04/26/08	Saturday	8:00 AM	5:00 PM		All	Business		**Validate Master Data (Manual Entry) II**	
23.1							PP	Bonnie		Work Centers	
23.2							PP	Bonnie		Routings	
23.3							PP	Bonnie		Batch Master - Load batch (Batch Master - Load batch)	NA
23.4							QM	Steve		Inspection Characteristics	
23.5							QM	Steve		Inspection Plans	

Step # 17, Master Data Objects Load in MBP: Once the configuration is in the BI production system, the relevant master data can be maintained in BI.

Step # 18, Manual BI Configuration: Configuration is then maintained in BI that was dependent on the master data objects.

Step # 19, STOP ALL TRANSACTIONS in Legacy System & Lock all users out of the legacy system (except FI): At this point, all users must stop posting transactions in the legacy system. In this case, the company runs on a 4-4-5 fiscal calendar, all fiscal periods end on a Friday. Therefore, this happens at noon on Friday of the cut-over weekend.

Step # 20, Complete all scheduled jobs in Legacy system: The idea is to complete the end-of-day shipping process, run the final customer invoices and run reports that will be used for comparing data to the SAP system for validation that all data was migrated properly. It is time to prepare for the financial close in the legacy system.

Step # 21, Begin FI Close: The Finance Users are now the only ones with access to the legacy system. They must quickly close the books for the last financial period in the legacy system. The financial close must be very fast; therefore we usually schedule the go-live at the end of the first or second period of a fiscal quarter. We try to avoid go-lives at quarter-end and always avoid go-lives on a year-end.

Step # 22, Schedule Background Jobs / Process Chains in SAP ECC & BI for the new site to start running upon go-live. It is a good practice to have a check list of background jobs that should be running for the new site in SAP.

Step # 23, Validate Master Data (Manual Entry) II: This is a follow-on activity from Step # 15. Once that data has been entered, it needs to be validated. In this example, it will be validated the day after it was entered.

Step # 24, Complete FI Closing: By Sunday at noon, the Financial Closing in the legacy system needs to be complete. It may be very difficult for companies to close their books in only 2 days, but it is essential for the cut-over. At this company,

Figure 11.4 Sample Cut-over Plan (steps 24 – 28)

Step	Pre	Date	Day	From (Time)	To (Time)	Area	Who	Status	Activity Description	Remarks
24.0		04/27/08	Sunday		Noon	FI	ALL Finance		Complete FI Closing	
25.0		04/27/08	Sunday	Noon	1:00 PM	IT	Amy		Run & Verify Full Backup of PCMRP	PCMRP
26.0	24.0	04/27/08	Sunday	1:00 PM	6:00 PM				Extract Open Data + Prepare for Upload or Manual Entry	
26.1						MM	Amy		Material Movement Last Transaction Date	PCMRP
26.2						MM	Amy		Inventory Balances	PCMRP
26.3						PP	Amy		Production Order Balances (added to Inv	PCMRP
26.4						FI	Denise		GL Account Balances - P7 beginning - P7 delta - P8 delta	manual spreadsheet
26.5						FI	Denise		Open A/P Balances as of P8	manual
26.6						FI	Denise		Open A/R Balances as of P8	manual
26.7						FI	Denise		Delta asset transactions in P7	
26.8						FI	Denise		Delta asset transactions in P8	
27.0	26.0	04/27/08	Sunday	2:00 PM	11:59 PM		Business		Validate + Adjust Open Data in Preparation for Upload	
27.1						MM	Liz		Material Movement Last Transaction Date	
27.2						MM	Liz		Inventory Balances	
27.3						PP	Liz		Production Order Balances (added to Inv	
27.4						FI	Denise		GL Account Balances - P7 beginning - P7 delta - P8 delta	manual spreadsheet
27.5						FI	Denise		Open A/P Balances as of P8	manual
27.6						FI	Denise		Open A/R Balances as of P8	manual
27.7						FI	Denise		Delta asset transactions in P7	
27.8						FI	Denise		Delta asset transactions in P8	
28.0	27.0	04/28/08	Sunday	12:00 AM	12:30 AM	All	All		Pre-Load Meeting (Go / No Go Decision)	End of Day

they will need to get used to closing fast because once they are on SAP, they will be performing the internal financial close in 3 days, which is our standard process (and a Best in Class performance according to the Hackett Group). Still this is very difficult for some to get used to so the champions from the Finance department of the sister site or Corporate will help them through it.

Step # 25, Run & Verify Full Backup of legacy system: This step is not essential to the projects but it is a good practice to run a backup of the legacy system once the Financial Close is complete.

Step # 26, Extract Open Data & Prepare it for Load or Manual Entry: Once the Financial Close is complete, we need to extract the open data and format it for load or entry into SAP. Each of these objects should be listed in sub steps.

Step # 27, Validate & Adjust Open Data in Preparation for Upload: The business users must validate the data that has been extracted and is ready to load into SAP. Adjustments may need to be made to the data to accommodate the account settings in SAP.

Step # 28, Pre-Load Meeting (Go / No-Go Decision): Once the data is validated, we have a quick meeting to determine if we are ready to load the data. We call this a Go / No-Go Decision meeting because once the open data is loaded in SAP, it is very hard to reverse. It will be easier to fix a problem in SAP than to revert back to a prior state. It would usually take longer to restore from back up and reload the data than fix the problem in SAP. We need to be sure that we are ready to go-live. If the decision is a "Go", it is time to load the open data.

It is good to note that the reason we did not show a step in the plan to back up the SAP system before we started is because there is already a full backup of the SAP environment performed nightly. If you do not already have a daily backup scheduled, then it would be prudent to include a step for this prior to loading open data.

I am proud to say that we have never had to make a "No-

Figure 11.5 Sample Cut-over Plan (steps 29 – 31)

Step	Pre	Date	Day	From (Time)	To (Time)	Area	Who	Status	Activity Description	Remarks
29.0	28.0	04/28/08	Monday	6:00 AM	6:00 PM	IT	Laks / Amy		**Open Data Load**	
29.1						IT	Laks / Amy		Inventory Balances	
29.2						IT	Laks / Amy		Production Order Balances (added to Inv Balances)	
29.3						IT	Laks / Amy		Material Movement Last Transaction Date	
29.4						IT	Laks / Denise		GL Account Balances - P7 beginning - P7 delta - P8 delta	
29.5						IT	Laks / Denise		Open A/P Balances as of P8	
29.6						IT	Laks / Denise		Open A/R Balances as of P8	
29.7						IT	Laks / Amy		Post delta asset transactions in P7 and Run Depreciation in P8	
29.8						IT	Laks / Amy		Post delta asset transactions in P8 and Run Depreciation in P8	
30.0		04/28/08	Monday	1:00 PM	4:00 PM	All	Business		**Open Data (Manual Entry)**	
30.1	27.6					MM	Bill / Jennifer		Purchase Orders	
30.2						SD	Monica		Sales Orders	
30.3						PP	Liz		Work Orders	
31.0	30.0	04/28/08	Monday	10:00 AM	9:00 PM	All	Business		**Validate Open Data Loaded + Manual Entry**	
31.1						MM	Liz		Material Movement Last Transaction Date	
31.2						MM	Liz		Inventory Balances	
31.3						PP	Liz		Production Order Balances (added to Inv Balances)	
31.4						FI	Denise		GL Account Balances - P7 beginning - P7 delta - P8 delta	
31.5						FI	Denise		Open A/P Balances as of P8	
31.6						FI	Michelle		Open A/R Balances as of P8	
31.7						FI	Denise		Asset Subledger as of P7	
31.8						FI	Denise		Asset Subledger as of P8	
31.9						MM	Bill		Purchase Orders	
31.10						SD	Monica		Sales Orders	

Go" decision. For each of these fast implementations, we have been prepared for the "Go" decision.

Step # 29, Open Data Load: As soon as the "Go" decision is made, we start loading the open data into SAP. Again the sub steps show each of the objects that will be loaded via a program.

Step # 30, Open Data (Manual Entry): The sub steps here list the data objects that will be loaded manually.

Step # 31, Validate Open Data: The users must validate the data that was loaded in SAP to ensure that it ties with the data that was in the legacy system upon completion of the financial close. Proof of this validation is documented for audit purposes.

Step # 32 & # 33, Close Period 8 and Open Period 9: Obviously the financial periods should reflect the actual periods as they pertain to your project. But in this example, period 8 is the fiscal month that has just closed. Period 9 is the new fiscal month that is about to start. Remember that we always implement SAP over a fiscal period end. The last transactions performed in the legacy system were performed in the previous month (period 8 in this example) and the finance department closed the last period in the legacy system. When we load that data in SAP, it is loaded in period 8. Once that data is loaded and validated, we need to open period 9 so new transactions are performed in the new financial period. In SAP, this must be done for both the Material period and the Fiscal period.

Step # 34, Pre Go-Live Meeting (Go / No-Go Confirmation): Prior to transporting the final configuration which will activate the new site, we have a meeting to ensure that all steps were followed and no show stoppers have cropped up.

Step # 35, Transport of Post Data Migration Configuration Settings: If the new site has local reporting requirements for taxes on fixed assets and you configured the system to handle this using a special depreciation area, the basis person needs to transport the final configuration to deactivate the special depreciation area after the open load is complete.

Figure 11.6 Sample Cut-over Plan (steps 32 – 41)

Step	Pre	Date	Day	From (Time)	To (Time)	Area	Who	Status	Activity Description	Remarks
32.0		04/28/08	Monday	9:00 PM		MM	Anil		Close Period 8 and Open Period 9	
33.0		04/28/08	Monday	9:00 PM		FI	Jing		Close Period 7 & 8 and Open Period 9	
34.0	31.0	04/28/08	Monday	11:00 PM	12:00 AM	All	All		Pre Go-Live Meeting (Go / No Go Confirmation)	
35.0						BASIS	Surendra G		Transport of Post Data Migration Config Settings	
36.0	31.0	04/28/08	Monday	11:00 PM	12:00 AM	All	All		** Final ECC Sign-off from Finance **	
37.0	38.0	04/29/08	Tuesday	12:01 AM		BASIS	Surendra G		Transport Activation Configuration Settings	
38.0	36.0	04/28/08	Monday	Midnight					Go-Live in SAP	
39.0	37.0	04/29/08	Tuesday	12:01 AM	1:00 AM	BASIS	Surendra G		Unlock users in MRP & MBP	
40.0		04/30/08	Wed	9:00AM	12:00NN		Cindy		Extract ECC data into BI-BCS	
40.1									- Collect period 7 for Adtron in LE and MA areas	
40.2									- Collect period 8 for Adtron in LE and MA areas	
40.3									- Verify balances thru BS and PL reports in both LE and MA areas	
41.0	40.3	04/30/08	Wed	12:00NN	5:00PM	All	Joanne / Gloria		** Final BI / BCS Sign-off from Finance **	

Step # 36, Final ECC Sign-off from Finance: Prior to Go-Live, get a final sign-off from the corporate controller or CFO and from the site controller after they have reviewed and agree that the financial account balances for the new company code are correct.

Step # 37, Transport Activation Configuration Settings: The last configuration settings can now be transported. They are to activate the new company code in FI and to activate the new company code in asset accounting (if you use asset accounting in SAP).

Step # 38, Go-Live: This is simply a milestone acknowledging that the system is in a live state.

Step # 39, Unlock users in SAP ECC and BI: The basis person can now unlock the users so they can begin transacting in the new company code in SAP and can access BI reports.

Step # 40, Extract ECC data into BI – BCS: Populate BI with new data loaded into the new company code in SAP. BCS (Business Consolidation System) is a component of BI that is used for financial consolidations. Financial data is populated in this module to roll up to corporate for closing the last fiscal period.

Step # 41, Final BI / BCS Sign-off from Finance: Once the data is populated in BI and BCS, the corporate controller or CFO and the site controller will sign-off that the data in our reporting tools are correct. This sign-off is important from a SOX audit perspective.

Weekend Warrior

Usually I copy a subset of the cut-over plan to a separate tab and use it when creating presentations. This section of the plan specifically covers weekend days and holidays that business users do not normally plan to be in the office. It is essential for certain people (key users, champions, and site managers) to be in the office to perform their steps in the cut-over plan.

We also need to ensure that the team working on the project will have access to the building during this cut-over weekend. Therefore, the plant manager and site security will need to be notified. Figure 11.7 shows a sample of a Weekend Warrior spreadsheet tab.

The cut-over plan will be slightly different for each implementation. But once you have the first one, it is easy to customize it for your project. For example, the sub steps for the data migration areas will be different depending on your decision on the data migration approach for each object. Steps will be added or removed based on which SAP applications you plan to roll out at one time. It also depends on your configuration requirements and local reporting requirements. Now you have a template, and you should be able to customize it to your needs within a couple of hours. The best way to get this done fast is to have a working meeting with a BSA from each module plus your basis / security person. You should, however wait until your configuration is complete (at least in DEV) and the decisions have been made on the data migration approach for each object.

Figure 11.7 Sample Weekend Warriors tab from the Cut-over plan workbook.

Date	Day	From (Time)	To (Time)	Area	Who	Status	Activity Description	Remarks
04/26/08	Saturday	8:00 AM		IT	All		Schedule Background Job/Process Chains in MRP & MBP	
04/26/08	Saturday	8:00 AM	5:00 PM	All	Business		Validate Master Data (Manual Entry) II	
				PP	Bonnie		Work Centers	
				PP	Bonnie		Routings	
				PP	Bonnie		Batch Master - Load batch (Batch Master - Load batch)	N/A
				QM	Steve		Inspection Characteristics	
				QM	Steve		Inspection Plans	
04/27/08	Sunday		Noon	FI	ALL Finance		Complete FI Closing	
04/27/08	Sunday	Noon	1:00 PM	IT	Amy		Run & Verify Full Backup of PCMRP	PCMRP
04/27/08	Sunday	1:00 PM	6:00 PM				Extract Open Data + Prepare for Upload or Manual Entry	
				MM	Amy		Material Movement Last Transaction Date	PCMRP
				MM	Amy		Inventory Balances	PCMRP
				PP	Amy		Production Order Balances (added to Inv Balances)	PCMRP
				FI	Denise		GL Account Balances -P7 beginning -P7 delta -P8 delta	manual spreadsheet
				FI	Denise		Open A/P Balances as of P8	manual spreadsheet
				FI	Denise		Open A/R Balances as of P8	manual spreadsheet
				FI	Denise		Delta asset transactions in P7	
				FI	Denise		Delta asset transactions in P8	
04/27/08	Sunday	2:00 PM	11:59 PM		Business		Validate + Adjust Open Data in Preparation for Upload	
				MM	Liz		Material Movement Last Transaction Date	
				MM	Liz		Inventory Balances	
				PP	Liz		Production Order Balances (added to Inv Balances)	
				FI	Denise		GL Account Balances -P7 beginning -P7 delta -P8 delta	manual spreadsheet
				FI	Denise		Open A/P Balances as of P8	manual spreadsheet
				FI	Denise		Open A/R Balances as of P8	manual spreadsheet
				FI	Denise		Delta asset transactions in P7	
				FI	Denise		Delta asset transactions in P8	
04/28/08	Sunday	12:00 AM	12:30 AM	All	All		Pre-Load Meeting (Go / No Go)	End of Day

Chapter 12
Go-Live

"Life is either a daring adventure, or nothing."

– Helen Keller

It's hard to beat the feeling of going live with SAP at a new manufacturing plant. Everything that you have worked so hard to accomplish in such a short amount of time culminates in the few moments that you realize you have done it – again. It is very exciting. Everyone on the team is excited. There are always some people amazed at what you have accomplished. They went along with the implementation on such a short time line, but they thought they would watch it fail. They thought that in the end you would have to push out the go-live at least a month or two. But it is at this moment that they are amazed that they have actually accomplished what they previously thought was impossible.

I am always extremely proud of the team. The SAP teams that I have assembled to roll out SAP following this approach are very proud of themselves at go-live and they should be. They are among a very elite few that have accomplished such a feat. You and your team could join the elite few by following this approach, the SMART Approach to implementing SAP.

Processing the first shipment and creating the first customer invoice is my favorite activity after go-live. I remember my first go-live very well. It was February 4, 1999 at

2:30 AM Pacific. The folks from the receiving department were on hand ready to receive the inventory that had piled up over a couple of days in the receiving department. By noon that day, I was in the war room and received a call from our key user in the shipping department. He was ready to ship the first shipment on SAP. I turned to our SD (Sales and Distribution) consultant and said, "They are ready to process the first shipment. Do you want to come out to the floor with me and watch?" He shrugged his shoulders replying, "Sure." We went out to the shipping floor and stood looking over the shoulder of the key user as he performed the packing and post goods issue transactions. The packing list printed automatically in the correct shipping lane. I slapped him on the back and said, "Good job!" Then I turned to the SD consultant and saw him standing there with his jaw practically touching the floor. I could see the whites of his eyes had grown larger than I had ever seen. I was concerned and asked, "What's wrong?" He stuttered a little and said, "N-nothing. It's just that I have never seen a company ship the first day they went live before." I could not believe what I had just heard him say. This man was a seasoned SAP consultant and he had never seen a company ship the first day they went live? I was astonished and suddenly very concerned. I had just realized that although we communicated a whole lot during the project, he never told me that he didn't expect to ship the first day, and I had never told him that we absolutely _had_ to. Our president and CEO promised Cisco Systems that we would ship product that day after being down for a couple of days during the cutover. I knew that if we did not ship that day, we could have lost one of our largest customers.

Afterwards, our CFO did some investigation and found that only about 20% of SAP customers shipped the first day they went live. That may have been true back in the late 90's by now I am sure the percentage must be much higher.

Since then, there has been a friendly competition between sites as we rolled out SAP. Each site wanted to ship earlier in the day than the last site. The next site to go live was Scotland

and they shipped by 10:30AM the morning they went live. Puerto Rico shipped by 9:30 AM. Penang had product staged to ship by 8:30 AM. By my 15th site implementation, we were ahead of schedule on the cutover plan and the plant manager wanted to break our shipping record so we decided to bring up SAP on Monday night rather than Tuesday morning when we had planned to go live. The plant manger was with us out on the shipping floor at 10:30PM when we shipped the first shipment. He boasted that they shipped their first shipment *before* they were scheduled to go-live! Therefore he beat the record of the 14 plants that were brought up on SAP before him.

Friendly competitions like this are healthy; each site trying to do better than the last. It is fun for them and it is good for the company.

The team undertakes much personal sacrifice to accomplish a 2 month implementation. They have a lot of sleepless nights and weekends when they had to work. With the team all going through these sacrifices together, this in itself builds a common ground. They spend a lot of time together. They eat together and work together, and when they have time, they share stories and laugh together. When they are done, they have succeeded together and they are all very proud of themselves. It is very important to take some time after the dust settles to celebrate - even if it is just a lunch. They deserve a bonus and some time off. They just saved the company hundreds of thousands of dollars compared to a normal SAP implementation.

Chapter 13
Post Go-Live Support

"Success, happiness, peace of mind and fulfillment, the most priceless of human treasures, are available to all among us, without exception, who make things happen, who make *good* things happen, in the world around them."

– Joe Klock

The team is now very tired after a long cut-over weekend where they had to work very long hours and dealt with some very tough decisions full of debates with business users and other team members. They have sifted through tons of data during the data migration and validation of open data. They helped people understand how SAP works and why data needs to be set up in a certain way. They have had to mold "AS-IS" business processes data into "TO-BE" processes and system settings. They have barely had any time to eat or sleep. They are exhausted and relieved that we went live on time. Now they deserve a break; maybe some time off - some comp time for the long hours. But the job is not over yet. The first couple of days are the toughest.

The BSAs and champions find themselves pulled in many directions. Everyone needs their help. Everyone is doing real transactions in SAP for the first time. It is somewhat chaotic, but the chaos is well-controlled because of the structure that we have put in place. The champions are on the front line. They are working side-by-side with the users. They are letting the users perform the transactions, but they are watching over their shoulders guiding them and answering questions along the way.

When the champions are cornered with questions they cannot answer, they call in the BSAs for help. Then the users and the champions learn together from the BSAs. The next time the champion comes across the same question, they will now be prepared to handle it on their own. Experiences like these make the champions even better at their jobs when they return home.

The project team stays on site during the first week. The second week after go-live the key users are on the front line. When the key users have questions, they call their champion buddy at the sister site. They are already used to working together during testing, training and the first week after go-live. The key users know that the champions do the same job at a different site and they have learned a lot from the champions throughout the project. This makes them the logical choice to call if they have a problem. If necessary, they can initiate a web meeting and walk through the screens together remotely. Again if the champions have trouble, they can lean on the BSAs. The BSAs maintain an issues log for all of the issues that have been raised to them.

This post go-live issues log is maintained for the first two weeks. Issues that come up after the first two weeks follow our normal incident and change management process. But in the first two weeks, the tracking is done in the post go-live issues log. Figure 13.1 shows a sample of a post go-live issues log.

Because the key users and champions were on the front line answering questions, the issues are well filtered before they reach the SAP team. This allows the SAP team deal with and log real issues rather than training issues. They can focus on issues that require adjustments to the configuration and data migration making sure that we can act swiftly to avoid major production delays.

This support structure is critical to having a well-executed 2 month SAP implementation. In a 2 month SAP implementation, mistakes happen, some things are over-looked.

Figure 13.1 Sample Post Go-Live Issues Log

Legend

Category: 1-Vendor Master, 2-Customer Master, 3-Material Master, 4-BOMB, 5-LSMW, 6-BDC, 7-, 8-

Priority: High, Medium, Low

Status: Open, Closed, Deferred

Number	Description of process	User	Date	IT-REQ#	Priority	Task assigned to	Problem Documentation Furnished?	Document?	Status	COMMENTS
1	90+ PO's were not loaded into SAP. This is due to 35 vendors NOT being added into SAP. Add vendors and re-process PO upload errors.	Iraida Rivera	10/03/02		High	Mario P / Lindsay C			Closed	The 35 vendors were manually entered into SAP. These vendors were entered into BAAN after data extracts were done. Re-processed load errors and cleared the problem.
2	Receipt Traveler for Receiving NOT printing	Carlos Ortiz	10/03/02		High	Mario P / Lindsay C			Closed	Receipt Traveler was configured to print by plant, changed it to print by Receiving Location
3	Receipt Traveler for MRO Items Received NOT printing. MRO items are not printing because they are NOT inventory items. Need to change receipt travelet configuration to print by Purchasing Group.	Carlos Ortiz	10/04/02		High	Mario P / Yong			Open	Mario to email Yong the user Ids and Yong will maintain the settings today.
4	PO Printer (P2PO) is too slow. The printer is an inkjet, need to change it to a laser printer.	Iraida Rivera	10/04/02		High	Mario P / Jeannette C			Open	Need to Replace all printers to network-ready printers. Mario will send this list to Andy Purba.
5	Item Master (Sales View) for all Aguadilla part numbers are missing "Loading Group". This causes that the shipping point defaults to 02 and packing lists are printing to Aguada.	Gladys Badillo	10/07/02		High	Mario P / Jeannette C			Open	Jeanette to determine which materials are missing the loading group 0011. If many, we will add it via BDC.

But the same is true in a 9 month SAP implementation. The benefits of a 2 month roll-out far outweigh the costs. Because the support structure is in place, issues that crop up can be resolved extremely quickly.

Several companies that took 6 month or longer to roll out SAP have had major production down issues upon go-live. I have never had a production down situation upon or after the go-live of a 2 month implementation. I attribute this success to having a good, lean team that uses templates and follows the plan. They have a positive attitude and they know the pitfalls to steer clear from. I attribute our success to the cookie-cutter approach and having a strong management team that understands the benefits of running the same processes throughout a global company. I attribute our success to the approach that I have developed over the years – the SMART Approach to implementing SAP.

When the dust settles, it is important to have the key users join the Champion Community. I consider the project as well as the first couple of post go-live weeks, to be the initiation for the key users. At this point they are full-fledged champions and they should join the town hall style meetings that the Champion Community participates in regularly throughout the life of the company.

Chapter 14
Project Documentation

"Hard work often leads to success. No work seldom does."
– Harvey Mackay

Some may argue that on such a quick implementation, there will be no time to document your changes. That is simply not true. I make the project manager responsible for collecting and maintaining all of the project documentation. For most implementations we end up with at least a 4" binder packed full of project documentation. Often we have more than that.

Prior to being mandated by Sarbanes-Oxley controls, we maintained a lot less documentation in hard copy and we are working with our SOX auditors to allow us to reduce the printed requirements and be more eco-friendly again. But whether or not you print the project documentation or keep it in soft form, it is definitely possible and a best practice to document all of your project work.

Below is an outline of documents that I maintain for an SAP implementation.

- Project Definition Document
- Project Approval Presentation
- IT Steering Committee meeting minutes showing approval of the project

- High Level Project Plan
- Project Kick-off Presentation
- Implementation Team Travel Schedule
- Buddy List
- Project Document
    - Outlines the purpose, scope and high-level configuration requirements.
    - Contains the Responsibilities and Measurements of success
- Business Blueprint Document
    - Contains the detailed configuration plans for each module
    - Contains To-Be process flows and how they relate to the configuration
- Detailed Project Plan
- Unit Tests (signed & dated by the SAP Team)
- Integration Tests (signed & dated by the key users & champions)
- Cut-over Plan
- Finance Sign-off Sheet for SAP R/3 / ECC (signed & dated by the Site Controller, the Site General Manager, and the Corporate Controller or the CFO)
- Finance Sign-off Sheet for BI & BCS (signed & dated by the Site Controller, and the Corporate Controller or the CFO)
- Email approval of Financial data load results
    - Copy of the GL balance report (signed & dated by the site controller)
- Role-to-User Sign-off (signed & dated by the Site Controller)
    - Includes supporting data
- Master Vendor Load Sign-off (signed & dated by the Site Controller & Director of Procurement)
- Fixed Assets Sign-off (signed & dated by the Site Controller)
    - Supporting assets list signed & dated by the Finance person who entered the records
- Customer Master file signed & dated by the Site Accounts Receivable Manager
- Customer Account Balance file signed & dated by the Site Accounts Receivable Manager
- QM Inspection Data signed & dated by the Site Quality Manager

Chapter 15
Lessons Learned

"Our lives improve only when we take chances – and the first and most difficult risk we can take is to be honest with ourselves."
                                        – Walter Anderson

There are many lessons that I have learned throughout the years on SAP implementations. Each implementation is different. The people are different, the business scenarios are different, the company's products and services are different, the food is different, the languages and/or accents are different, the climate is different, the war rooms are different, and people's attitudes are different. But the implementation approach and the results are the same.

It is important at the end of each project to step back and document the detailed lessons learned to avoid facing the same problems during the next implementation. I take the time to update the project plan and the cutover plan that I will use as templates for the next implementation. It is difficult to find the time to do this. There are always post-implementation support issues and production issues to deal with. There is always a backlog of projects and pressure to complete them. But you must make the time to document lessons learned after each project. By doing this, you get better with each implementation.

What I Have Learned

What is amazing to me is the amount of work that can be accomplished in such a short amount of time. Over the years we continued to add more business process and more SAP modules and components to our environment. We have added the compliance components such as SAP GRC® and GTS®. The GRC (Governance, Risk, and Compliance) component includes Compliance Calibrator and the Access Enforcer workflow tool which helps keep our systems free of SOD (Segregation of Duties) violations. The GTS (Global Trade Server) component helps to ensure that we ship products in accordance with embargo laws. It screens our shipments for countries, companies and individuals that we should not be shipping to. We have added BW for analytics, BCS® (Business Consolidation System) for financial consolidations, and EP (Enterprise Portals) as an Intranet as well as a customer and supplier portal application. We also added SAP APO (Advanced Planning Optimization) and SAP PI® as a middleware.

As we added these applications, we included them (and the processes they support) in our new site implementations – and still we could do it all following a 2 month project plan!

In addition to strong executive support, there are 10 elements to a successful 2 month implementation. You can think of them as ingredients to the secret sauce of my success.

The ingredients of success:

1. Keep the SAP Team Small
2. The Buddy System
3. The Sister Site
4. Standard Global Business Processes
5. Single Global Instance of Each Application
6. Standard Configuration Set
7. Use Templates for Everything
8. Start the Data Migration Early
9. Be Careful with the Use of Sandboxes
10. Humor

1. Keep the SAP Team Small

I mentioned this in Chapter 3 "Project Preparation", but it is worth repeating. It is important to keep the SAP team small. Even in the original implementation of a very large organization, a smaller team will get the core configuration done much faster than a large team. SAP is extremely configurable. There are many ways to achieve the required results. If there are 5 MM (Materials Management) BSAs in the room, there will probably be 6 or more ideas under debate on how to configure sub-contract purchase orders. In other words, make sure there are not too many cooks in the kitchen. A small team is both more productive and obviously less expensive. You need a small team of experts who each know their module /component very well.

2. The Buddy System

We have already reviewed the Buddy System in Chapter 3 "Project Preparation", as well. I cannot stress how effective this is. Complimenting your SAP team with champions who are the buddies of your key users is instrumental. The champions are the business process experts. They do the job day in and day out. They know the pitfalls and they know all of the short cuts. No matter how well the BSAs know the business processes, the champions know them better. There is no better person to train new users than the champion. There is no better support person for the new users than the champion. The new site will come up to speed much faster, if they have people to lean on who are already doing the same job in the same way.

The champions take a lot of pressure off the SAP team and champions are less expensive than SAP experts. Over the years, I have managed projects that utilized the Buddy System and projects that did not utilize the Buddy System. I guarantee that you will have much greater success utilizing the Buddy System.

3. The Sister Site

It is a good idea to have the key users from the new site visit the sister site prior to go-live. They will see firsthand how the business processes work. It will give them a very good idea of how it should work at their site. Seeing a business process on paper is much different than seeing it in action. You can get an understanding of the process on paper, but when you see it in action you learn the details that you don't always see on paper. You see when and how forms are used and you see real life examples of how they are filled out. You see the physical layout of the facility and the best practices in place. The key users should bring home the ideas they have seen in practice at the sister site and get ready to put them into action at their site.

During the project, they will be able to relate to the discussions much easier and visualize the outcome much easier if they have seen how the sister plant operates. It is also a good idea to continue this practice after go-live. The more people that visit sister sites, the better the communication will be between them and the closer the business processes will remain aligned.

4. Standard Global Business Processes

It is a best practice for all sites within an organization to run a set of standard business processes. The benefits of this are almost countless and earlier in the book I outlined several of them. This is critical to becoming a world-class organization. Companies such as McDonald's and Wal-Mart have mastered this. This is, however, extremely difficult to achieve. Even with a mandate from the senior most executives, the act of business process agreement and alignment is extremely difficult and cumbersome. However, a global SAP implementation gives you the golden opportunity implement standard business processes. It may never be this easy again, so you must take advantage of the opportunity while you have it.

Still as you know, it is never _easy_ to standardize business processes, but now is the time to take a stand. Consider all of the different product lines and all of the different scenarios and determine a single way to handle each. Get the appropriate buy-in from the senior executives, configure SAP with that in mind and say, "This is the process approved by corporate" or "This is the way we do it in SAP."

If you come across a site that has a better business process, take note. Roll out your existing corporate approved process. Then, after the implementation, when the dust settles, take steps to roll out the better business process to all of your locations. This is easier said than done, but it is imperative to become a best in class organization.

I have led IT for companies through implementations and through the aftermath into the support stage for years. I know how difficult it is to keep the same business processes in practice throughout all sites. Many may not realize this, but the IT Applications department or what I like to call the Business Applications department plays a huge role in maintaining business process alignment over time. Requests for changes come from employees, customers, and suppliers all over the world. Usually these people are thinking about the change as one that they need for their site or their department or even for a specific customer. The Applications team needs to view the change in light of how it will impact the configuration and if there are other business units that would benefit from the same change. They need to explain the global ramifications of the change to the requestor and obtain buy-in from the other sites or business units. When the new functionality is tested, it needs to be tested for the other scenarios at the other sites or in the other business units that may benefit from it. This coordination usually adds time and requires more effort but the business benefits are enormous. If you cannot put a Design Review Committee in place to ensure this cohesion, then you at least need a QA step in the process prior to moving changes to your production SAP systems. Appoint a senior manager to be the global business process owner for each business area. These

BPOs will need to approve changes to business processes in their area. These global business process owners may be the same as the business data owners (BDOs) who approve user access to SAP for their respective business process areas. These approvers can be set up in SAP's GRC (Governance, Risk, and Compliance) workflow.

Not only will this help you the next time you acquire a company, but it will help keep your company in SOX (Sarbanes-Oxley Act, section 404) compliance. Or rather it will help keep your SOX compliance costs low.

Keeping the Global Champion Community active will also help to keep business processes standardized across all sites. If the Champion Community meets regularly, the result is continuous business processes improvement at a global level. Keeping the Champion Community active is difficult, but very important. Therefore, you should put someone in charge of organizing the meetings and taking notes and distributing them.

5. Single Global Instance of Each Application

Many companies have an instance of their ERP system at each manufacturing plant. This is how many companies were originally set up. However, if each site has their own instance of SAP, many problems arise. They end up using different fields to hold similar information or they end up with common fields used to hold different information. This results in reporting nightmares. It also turns into a huge project each time you want to move the manufacturing of a product or product line from one site to another. Employees from different sites who are trying to communicate to each other have to explain simple things in great detail for all to understand the situation at hand. This is not very productive.

Some may think allowing each site to have their own system is the easy way out. Employees from different sites do not have to agree on anything. They can each have it their own way. But if you think about it, this does not lead to a very efficient organization. I do not know of any companies organized this way that can roll out SAP to a manufacturing plant in 2 months. Not only do they lose synergies of the sites working seamlessly together, they also have much duplication in hardware and in staff; not only in IT staff but in other departments as well. This kind of disorganization has led some companies to outsource many of their departments in order to centralize business processes and decrease headcount. I believe a better solution is to standardize business processes across all sites. This will also allow companies to easily centralize functions, reduce headcount, but keep core business processes in house and keep operating costs low.

Some companies have regional instances of SAP. From the perspective of a rollout of SAP to the sites in that region, I think it is still possible to undertake 2 month implementations based on a regional standard configuration and set of business processes. However, it still makes it difficult for global reporting and transferring product lines and people from region to region.

I believe the best footprint is a single global instance of each application. This makes product line transfers and global reporting much easier. It promotes global awareness of business processes and procedures. Global telecommunications in this day and age is no longer an issue. If the hardware and network are sized appropriately, transaction response time is still measured in tenths of a second or even milliseconds.

The downside is that it is difficult to find down-time for software and server maintenance because it seems that someone is always working somewhere in the world. But I believe the pros far outweigh the cons for a single global instance of each application. I have worked for companies where all applications were a single global instance except for the MES system. Plants need access to their Manufacturing Execution System around the clock. If the link between the ERP and the MES system is temporarily down, they can still manufacture if the MES system is local. Today even when a communications link goes down, it is usually back up very quickly. Years ago, we had a lot of down time due to local telecom issues in some remote parts of the world, but even those occurrences have diminished greatly over the last few years.

6. Standard Configuration Set

This goes hand-in-hand with maintaining Standard Global Business Processes. If you have a standard set of business processes, then you should maintain a standard set of configuration for all sites. This keeps your IT costs low because you need fewer IT staffers. It keeps project complexity low because you need fewer IT project team members. It keeps development costs low because the application complexity is low. This is critical for an implementation following the SMART Approach. If the SAP configuration is the same for all sites, then the only configuration that needs to be performed during the implementation is the organizational settings (the company code, plant, sales organization, etc. and the assignments thereto). This will save an enormous amount of time during the project. Maintaining a standard configuration set is not easy, but I have covered the suggestions on how to do this in ingredient # 4, Standard Global Business Processes, above.

7. Use Templates for Everything

I look at the use of templates much like SOA. The concept of Service-Oriented Architecture is to develop reusable components. The idea is that it will speed up the development of future software products because you can reuse code or function modules that were previously created. This also standardizes the way code is written so it will be easy for future developers to modify to keep up with new business process requirements.

Templates are used in the same way, but applied to SAP implementations. Throughout this book I have talked about and illustrated several templates that I use in the SMART Approach to implementing SAP. Starting with templates that were used in previous projects will shave a significant amount of time off an SAP implementation. In fact, I believe that the use of templates contributes the most time savings to a project than anything else except the use of standard business processes and standard configuration across the enterprise.

I recommend using templates for project documents such as:
- The introductory packet
- The project budget
- The high level project plan
- The kick-off meeting presentation
- The detailed project plan
- The cut-over plan
- The unit test scripts
- The integration test scripts
- The test schedules
- The training schedules
- The travel schedules
- The training materials
- The issues logs
- The data migration maps
- The buddy list

8. Start the Data Migration Early

The data migration is one of the most critical and time consuming steps of the project. It in itself could take the entire 2 months. It is an activity that is done in parallel with the other activities. The project manager needs to keep a close eye on progress of the data migration from the extracts of the data objects from the legacy system, through the data mapping and test data loading. Problems with data migration could be a show stopper. I recommend starting as early as possible and hold regular updates on the progress throughout the project.

9. Be Careful with the Use of Sandboxes

After the initial SAP implementation is complete, I see no real need to maintain sandbox environments.

Some companies use sandboxes or test systems to develop and test new functionality before they repeat it in the golden development system. These sandboxes are isolated systems that allow a project team to perform their configuration in a place that is protected from other changes in the development environment. This sounds like a good idea, but I have been burned by using sandboxes. From that experience I realized that it is not necessarily the best solution. The problem is that most companies cannot afford to put all development of new functionality on hold while rolling out SAP to a new site. Although it seems like 2 months is not a long time to put development on hold, the reality is that the business continues to operate and innovate. We must be able to do multiple things at once. We have to be able to roll out changes while other projects are going on. A sandbox is an isolated environment. When you develop functionality in a sandbox, then move it to the golden development system, the configuration in the golden system may have changed to keep up with business requirements. The new configuration from your project in the sandbox may not be compatible with those business changes. This causes your project to be delayed while you reconfigure.

Personally I would rather know upfront if project configuration clashes with other changes. That way it can be addressed immediately and there will be no surprises requiring re-work. I have run SAP environments for years with no sandboxes. I believe it is the fastest way to innovate with the least amount of risk.

The only way a sandbox can be effective is if it is kept up-to-date with configuration changes that are released from the development environment. If your sandbox gets out of sync with other development activities, there will be an increased probability of problems and potential delays.

10. Humor

I have learned that humor is one of the best tools in your tool belt. Humor helps to break the ice when delivering presentations and updates to the management and to the user community. Humor lightens the mood if configuration discussions get heated between BSAs. Humor alleviates pressure during tense debates on business processes with the key users. I do not condone humor when it is aimed towards a person (other than one's self). The humor that I am talking about is not the kind that will make people feel stupid or the kind that down-plays someone's ideas or beliefs. The humor should be aimed at the situation, not at people. It is also important to recognize when humor is not working, and the situation requires a serious tone. It depends on the people you are working with or talking to in each individual discussion. Personalities play a large part in teamwork and the way you approach someone will make all of the difference in the world. Some project managers lead with an iron fist. This may, however, make for a long dark project with many ill feelings and mistrust that could jeopardize the success of a project. I have found that leading with a lighter tone draws much more productivity from the team. People who like to work with you will go the extra mile for you. They will not fight you every step of the way. People who have fun on the job are more productive, and on a 2 month implementation, the team needs to be at the peak of performance.

The combination of humor and experience is a winning combination. Humor makes people comfortable approaching you, while sharing your experience gives people the confidence that you know what you are doing. You need to be approachable. You need people to bring forward their concerns. They need to know they can bring up potential issues and voice concerns without being made fun of. Answering their questions and resolving their issues comes with experience. Talking about how similar issues were resolved at other sites gives people confidence in your experience. The project is tough enough and it is made bearable by having a little fun along the way. Combining a light and humorous tone with the experience that you have gained performing quick implementations is a key to success.

Success breeds success. Once you try it and are successful, your team will gain the confidence that they need to do it again and again.

I do not recommend doing these implementations back-to-back. I recommend at least one month in between. Two weeks will be post go-live support and having an additional two weeks of steady-state is important before, marching off to your next implementation. Therefore, you should be able to implement SAP at one manufacturing plant per quarter per team.

I am already thinking about how I would take lessons learned with this approach and applying them to implementations on a much larger scale. If large companies need to roll out SAP to 30 sites, this approach would take one team seven and a half years. A team working that long under such extreme conditions would be burned out way before completion. And companies should not have to wait that long to be able to take advantage of the synergies they will gain by having all sites on a single instance of SAP. The approach to a large-scale implementation will give me something else to write about in a future book.

The most valuable lesson I learned is that this SMART Approach is repeatable with different teams. Quite some time had passed between our previous 2 month implementation and our most recent acquisition. We had dealt with a divestiture, going public, preparing for Sarbanes-Oxley audits, rolling out

SAP APO, etc. We acquired a company on February 15th, held the kick-off meeting on March 3rd, and brought them live on SAP on April 28th.

During this implementation, I was in the war room discussing the specifics of the plan with the team and one of them was a little skeptical. I looked over to the MM/PP/QM BSA and asked, "You were with us when we did the implementation in China, right? You remember how it was." He responded, "No, I was not yet with the company." So I turned to the FI/CO BSA and asked, "Well, you were with us when we implemented in Korea. You remember, right?" She responded, "No. I was not here yet either." I looked around the room at the rest of the SAP team and the champions and realized that I was the only one in the room that had been through a 2 month implementation before. There was one other person on the team, our SD BSA, who had been through some 2 month implementations, but she did not travel with us. She was working on the project remotely because she was expecting her first child. She coordinated with the champion who was on site. The two of them worked together and did an outstanding job! I was also grooming a new project manager during this project that had not yet been through an implementation using the SMART Approach.

It was at that moment I realized that this approach is repeatable regardless of the team. Of course the SAP team has to be a seasoned team and they have to know the standard corporate processes. But I realized that a 2 month implementation could be performed by any seasoned team who follows the SMART Approach. As long as you have a positive attitude and are willing to try this approach, you can be successful as well.

With this revelation, it occurred to me that consulting companies that offer "out-of-the-box" SAP solutions can make this work as well, even for fast ERP implementations. Their community of customers could be their champion community.

When following this SMART Approach, it did not matter what products or services the newly acquired company offered, we were able to follow the approach and we were successful. This leads me to believe that out-of-the-box industry solutions should be successful as well. The customers of the solution just need to trust in the approach and let go of some of their existing business processes and be open to implementing industry best practices.

Acknowledgements

"At times our own light goes out and is rekindled by a spark from another person."

– Albert Schweitzer

There are many people to whom I owe much gratitude. Many of these people have rekindled my light when my spirits were down.

First and foremost, I consider myself to be the luckiest man in the world to be supported by my loving wife, Karen and our three beautiful daughters, Sarah, Michelle and Amanda. It is amazing to me that I still have a family life. The most stressful time in my career was when I was implementing SAP for the first time. I spent most of the time out of town. Unfortunately this was when our children were very young and my wife probably needed me the most. I am glad that everything seems to have worked out for the best and I am amazingly still married and have a wonderful family life.

The rekindling spark that I received from Ajay Birla was often more like an electric shock. I owe it to Ajay and to Wayne Eisenberg (who I reported to when I worked in Sales) for offering me the opportunity to make the transition from the business side to the IT department during my first SAP implementation. Wayne was one of the best managers / mentors I ever had, and I appreciate all that he has done for me.

As Ajay promoted me from a Business Systems Analyst to a Project Manager, he encouraged me to (or should I say demanded that I) find a way to implement SAP within 2 months to newly acquired manufacturing plants. With these achievements, Ajay promoted me to SAP Applications Manager and later to Director of IT Applications. Therefore, I am very grateful to Ajay Birla for the opportunities that he afforded me and the drive that he instilled upon me. He gave me goals that seemed impossible; and in the accomplishment of those goals I proved to myself that I could achieve amazing things if I applied myself.

I am also grateful to Ajay Shaw, who was a founder and the President and CEO of SMART Modular Technologies during the ERP decision. I think at one point, Ajay Shaw said, "SAP over my dead body!" Back in the late 1990s there were several companies that reported troubled SAP implementations which received a lot of press. One of our largest customers had an implementation nightmare so I understood his point. But all of the people at SMART that were involved in the comparison between ERPs agreed the SAP was the right choice for SMART, and Ajay agreed to proceed. Without this decision, my career would not have led me down the SAP path. A major influencer of this decision was our financial controller, Jack Pacheco.

Jack Pacheco was the CFO when SMART divested from Solectron. Jack was also one of the best managers I ever had. After the divestiture, when I was leading the IT Applications department, I reported to Jack. He and Iain MacKenzie, the new President and CEO of SMART Modular, supported my IT strategies and vision of migrating to and maintaining a single global instance of all enterprise applications on a single application platform. It was Shai Aggassi of SAP (at the time) who introduced me to the concept, but it was Jack and Iain that supported me in my efforts to make it a reality at SMART Modular Technologies. It takes a strong management team backing up the IT executives when rolling out a single global instance and requiring that all entities conform to a standard set of business processes. I appreciate all of the support that I received from Jack and Iain and I know they appreciated the results.

Srini Tanikella deserves more than honorable mention.

Srini was my IT Applications Manager. He is extremely skilled and talented. He became an official SAP Mentor. He helped us out of many practically impossible situations. He has become a good friend and a good leader. I appreciate all of the support he has given me.

When acknowledging people's contributions to SAP projects, I would be negligent not to show my sincere gratitude to the SAP team members that throughout the years actually made it all happen. Indy Banipal, Gottfried Burgmair, Wagner Canto, Vibol Chea, Kenneth Chong, Laura (Bradley) Cornwallis, the late Jeannette Cupeles, may she rest in peace. Ross Forman, Surendra Gannamaneedi, Shree Garga, Bernd Gemeinhardt, Pallavi Gupta, Antonia Habereder, David Harkin, Amy Horton, Larry Jin, Laura Johanson, Sanjay Kadam, Sukdev Kaloor, Thiru Karpur, Anil Kumar, Chau Yong Lim, Gokul Muthuswamy, Lindsay (Klein) Neill, Mario Perezalonso, Satya Prakash, Narinder Prashar, the late Mindie Prom (Thida Ea), may she rest in peace. Georg Reitmeier, Sandy Rojas, Goetz Salewski, Sridar Sarva, Gerhardt Schultz, Thilo Segerer, Balaji Shanmugam, Erna (Kottlowk) Stanglemayr, Jing Tulio, Laks Yelugoti and many more.

There are dozens of key users, champion users, and business managers that were a tremendous help to the success of our projects. I cannot name them all, but a few that stand out include: Bob Benkendorf, Louisa Camacho, David Castro, Maria DeJesus, Alan Fitzgerald, Bert Garcia, Jamie Horton, Bobby Jackson, Dr. Frank Jeschonnek, Vejay Kumar, Horia Leonescu, Joanne Leung, Steven Lyall, Frank McKane, Jeff Milano, Barry Needham, Katie (Reed) Pond, Anjali Reddy, Mike Robinson, Liz Sadlo, Dennis Scherbing, Colleen Seal, Barb Simental, Mohan Sivasankar, Bryan Smith, Celia Torres, Ashok Vaid, Josef Wenzl, Suzanne Woodhouse, and Gloria Zemla.

There are also some consultants that really stand out and deserve recognition. Frederick (Frikky) Koen, taught me how to configure the Sales & Distribution module. He was the best instructor. He helped me to think through the way to find configuration nodes and troubleshoot SAP configuration issues.

He opened my eyes to potential careers relating to the SAP platform. I will forever be in his debt.

David Osei-Yaw furthered what Frikky has started enlightening me on SAP configuration.

Venkat Seshadri is has been a great SAP mentor to me. He has always been there for me and I truly appreciate all of his help over the years. Venkat has become a great friend.

Craig Hammond has been an excellent life coach. I appreciate all of Craig's excellent advice and I truly enjoy hearing of his experiences in different industries.

I would also like to thank my friends at SAP. Grant Bodley and Mark David encouraged me to write this book. Roger Quinlan and Gary Primeau have always been very supportive.

I am particularly grateful Iain MacKenzie, CEO of SMART Modular Technologies, for authorizing the use of examples depicted in this book which I used on projects while at SMART Modular Technologies.

Thank you all.

"A man can succeed at almost anything for which he has unlimited enthusiasm."

– Charles Schwab

ABOUT THE AUTHOR

Dan Raven is a Global Information Technology professional with over 15 years of hands-on business experience designing, evaluating, installing and managing IT and software applications for leading global companies. Cited as a world class change agent, Dan has helped companies reduce operating cost while achieving higher efficiencies throughout their organizations. He has assembled and led multi-national teams in fast-paced environments. At the time this book was written, Dan had 15 SAP implementations under his belt and successfully followed the plan detailed in this book during 10 of those 15 SAP implementations.

"Enjoy the journey; there is no destination - only notable milestones along the way."

– Dan Raven

Made in the USA
Lexington, KY
12 May 2018